Latecomers to Love

Online Dating for Mature Men and Women:

First Online Meet-up Impressions

From a Man and a Woman

By: Dee Cleary & Bruce Miller

Published by: Pacific Trust Holdings NZ Ltd.

Contents

Introduction

Have you ever wondered what goes through a man's and a woman's mind when you first meet?

Have you ever asked yourself these questions?

"Why didn't he ask me out again?"

"Why doesn't she want to go out with me?"

"What did she think of me?"

"Am I too old, or too young, too dumb, too smart, etc. etc...?"

In "Latecomers to Love" you'll find answers to these questions in these interesting, amusing and saucy stories, drawn from the romantic lives of a couple of mature daters.

Online dating, and dating in general, particularly for those over the age of 50, can be awfully intimidating, especially when you've been in a relationship for a long time, and suddenly realize you hope to meet a new life partner.

When Bruce found himself newly single after an unwanted divorce, he followed the advice of a good friend who told him, "It's just a game of numbers." Bruce retired early and had time to meet many women and enjoyed meeting new ladies.

Dee too started a single life not long after turning 50, and, despite being intimidated by the idea, ventured onto the dating scene.

We hope our impressions of the fascinating, fun, interesting and at times, downright odd people we met will amuse and entertain you. Names and places have been changed for privacy.

"I change my mind so much, I need two boyfriends and a girlfriend."
- Pink

Chapter 1. DOREEN

Doreen's profile interested me. She was an avid golfer like me. We arranged to meet at a café midway between us and she walked in wearing jeans, a jean top, and rubber boots over flat tennis shoes.   She was attractive and had a great figure.

I stood up as she walked in, gave her a friendly kiss on the cheek, pulled out her chair and we ordered our coffees as she removed her rubber boots. Since I was dressed smart casual, I apologized for overdressing.

"I had to work in my garden this morning and the time got away from me so I did a "come as you are." She said.

"You're a very beautiful woman. I'd like to see what you look like when you clean yourself up!"

She laughed and we relaxed over the incongruence of our clothes. We gave each other a brief history of our lives and I learned she had a 20-year-old daughter who was getting married. Her husband had divorced her years ago and the wedding and reception were to take place at her home located on six acres in the country. She was getting her garden in showcase order while working on all the details for the upcoming wedding with 200 guests, all happening in two short months. We got along at our first coffee date and we continued to see each other.

Three weeks later, she asked me to go out to dinner with her family to celebrate her birthday. Her family were very welcoming and we talked easily - mostly about the upcoming wedding.

"He'll do Mom." Her daughter said unexpectedly while casually looking at me.

Puzzled, I didn't say anything. I looked over to Doreen and she was smiling.

"What?" I said.

"Oh, my daughter wants me to have an escort at her wedding."

"Fine with me." I said. I nodded a "Thank you" to her daughter.

"Mom, Bruce can help you with the outdoor canopy and all the tables."

"Oh, putting me to work already?" I laughed. "I would love to help you." All continued talking about the wedding. It was great fun over the next several weeks preparing for it and meeting Doreen's extended family and friends who also pitched in to help with setting up Doreen's country home for the wedding.

We worked hard most every day. I thought both of us needed a break so I asked Doreen if she'd be interested in playing a round of golf with me and a good friend of mine, Jim, an average golfer like me. She agreed and we all met at my golf club. We discussed having another lady to join us, but no one was available.

"So you're going to let a lady beat us both today." Jim remarked as Doreen split the fairway with her drive off the first lady's tee. Jim, a very wealthy business man, was in a great mood and was playing very well that day - far better than his usual game. Jim liked Doreen and I could see an attraction growing between them. Jim was married so I wasn't threatened and was glad they were getting along well.

Doreen was playing great too, but I was finding every sand trap and hazard on the course. Their unexpected camaraderie started getting to my head, which wasn't good for me since golf is a game that's played between your ears and you must keep a calm and positive mental attitude. While I kept struggling to get out of sand traps or rough, Doreen and Jim were joking and laughing while waiting for me.

My mind began to exaggerate their golf romance. When Doreen sunk a putt to finish a hole, she would slowly face Jim, and then bend over, picking her ball out of the cup in slow motion. Jim was getting a front row show of her cleavage each time.

We had drinks and lunch after the round and their attraction was still growing. I didn't know where this was going.

"You two are getting along well. I'm glad you're all having a good day." I said.

"Let's all play at my club the next time." Jim suggested.

"What club is that?" Doreen asked.

"The Orange Tree Club."

Okay, I thought. Jim's wife didn't golf and I surmised I was becoming a third wheel. A few days later, Jim and I talked.

"You better be careful with Doreen." He said.

"Why?" I asked.

"While you were having trouble on the course, she said to me, "I hope Bruce isn't holding his breath for a long-term relationship with me.""

"Shit! I was starting to like her. Hell, I've taken on working on her daughter's wedding." I said.

"I'm just telling you what she said, my good friend."

"Thanks, Jim. I appreciate that."

"You watched my back many times." Jim added.

"Why the hell do all the girls go for an ugly guy like you?" I joked.

"I've just got it." He laughed.

I called Doreen the next day and not wanting to let her know Jim repeated what she told him, I told her I couldn't come to her daughter's wedding because something unexpected came up. She started to cry over the phone.

"We need you. I need you." She pleaded, repeating things I had agreed to help with, adding "How are we going to get those done now on short notice?"

Her tears, or most any woman's tears, open doors for most men. I told her I would see what I could do to get out of it and help with the wedding.

Reluctantly, I kept my promise to help with the wedding and had a good time. Doreen and I danced the evening away.

Not wanting to do a fool me twice routine, after the wedding, I didn't date Doreen very much. Jim got divorced a year later and I wasn't surprised when he told me he and Doreen were seeing each other.

Dee's comments on Doreen:

Bruce, Bruce, Bruce.

Golf was not the only game being played on the green that day. It was a decider game and Jim and Doreen decided right there and then!

- Dee

"I'm a rich man, but I don't want to be a miser."
- Chen Guangbiao

Chapter 2. ROBERT

The prospect of dating, following a divorce in my fifties, after a long marriage, was very intimidating, but I felt I was still too young to spend the rest of my life alone.

"Get on the internet" my friends urged. "That's where it's at these days. Everyone's online dating!"

I wasn't quite convinced they knew what they were talking about, considering they all were firmly married or in long term relationships, but after several awkward occasions where I was set up with their dead-loss brothers or just-given-up-the-drugs male friends, I decided I couldn't do much worse by signing up to Match.com.

When Robert sent me a message asking if I'd be interested in communicating with him, I checked his profile. He was a bit older than I preferred, but seemed to be a fit and active guy, playing tennis and golf several times each week. He wrote well, with a touch of humor, and from his photo looked rather nice.

We corresponded for a short time, and then agreed to meet for coffee. I arrived a little early, so I was sitting in my car when he passed on his way to the coffee shop. He looked quite a bit older than his photo, and wore a grumpy expression, which made me laugh. Somehow I suspected he might not be the man of my dreams.

I followed him into the coffee shop and introduced myself, and we went to the counter. Robert politely ushered me forward to order my coffee, then said "I'll have the same".

"Would you like anything else?" he enquired, so I ordered a muffin, and he did too.

There wasn't any sign of his wallet being withdrawn from his pocket, so I ended up paying for the coffee and the cake for both. I didn't mind paying half, I was new to this dating game, so didn't know the rules, but I was a little surprised he hadn't offered to pay anything.

I did enjoy our meeting though, as contrary to the grumpy expression, Robert was quite amusing and made me laugh, he was quite fun. I like an adventurous man, and he told me he'd spent four days walking in the forests of Thailand, which impressed me.

Robert contacted me again and this time took me to dinner at an Indian restaurant. He bought me a rose from a passing vendor, which was a nice, romantic gesture and even nicer, he did pay his share this time.

On our third date, we went to a movie, but as he couldn't find a car-park, Robert suggested I go in and buy the tickets while he found a park. He came into the theatre just as I was paying, but didn't offer to share the cost. I thought 'Oh well", and bought ice-creams for us both, as I didn't want to be mean, and I wanted one.

After the movie, Robert suggested dinner and we went to a small local restaurant nearby. We had an enjoyable time, but when we left, I foolishly offered a hundred dollar note for my share of the $60 meal. Robert promptly said 'Thank you very much', and pocketed the change! Hmm.

"Excuse me, I think that's mine". I wasn't letting him away with it this time.

"Oh?" he reluctantly withdrew his hand, and I could see it pained him as he placed the notes in mine.

He drove me home and we arrived just as my daughter pulled up. I introduced her to Robert, he chatted politely, then made his excuses and left.

"What do you think?" I asked my daughter. I didn't want to tell her my negative thoughts about him, she already disapproved of my going out into the world of dating, but I was definitely going off Robert.

"Mom!" she said. "He walks like an old man and wears his pants up to his armpits!"

Oh, dear, this was the killer blow. Even the ex-drug-addicts were beginning to look slightly better in hindsight.

An unanswered invitation from Robert was sitting in my emails when my friend, Carol, told me Robert had contacted her on the same dating site, and invited her out. I could see why. Carol is a very sexy lady.

"Should I warn her he's a little careful with his money?" I wondered, but then remembered Carol was equally proficient at extracting expensive gifts from men, and encouraging them to spend a great deal of money on her.

"Now don't get offended if he prefers me", she giggled. "You know how popular I've always been with the guys".

I did indeed. How could I forget the number of boyfriends she'd enticed away from me in High School?

"You go right ahead, and do have a nice time" I smiled sweetly. "I really think you two are a match made in heaven!"

Bruce's Comments on Robert:

Dearest Dee,

You don't understand the genius of this frugal man and you need to disregard the cobwebs on his wallet.

You could have easily won his heart and wrapped him around your beautiful little finger if you only thought of these points:

1. Suggest meeting in a hotel lobby where you could have gotten for free two instant coffee packets and brought hot water in a thermos bottle and paper cups in a large handbag.

2. For muffins, next time check the dumpsters of various cafes on your way to the hotel too! Be sure to hold your nose when you dive in looking for a clean one.

Remember, most men love women who are frugal and instinctively run like a bat out of hell when they hear, "Oh, Robert, buy me this!" He would have fallen deeply in love with you.

As far as his taste in clothes, only the smartest of men wear their pants up to their armpits, as it makes pickpockets look for easier prey.

By the way, Carol asked me how you were while she was cleaning her 38 caliber Taurus hammerless 5 shot revolver. Don't worry, I will keep an eye on your back.

Better luck next time!

-Bruce

"Some foolish men continue to argue with a female until they realize they can never win. A woman will never give up and will keep going until she has the last word or has pissed you off."
- Anonymous

Chapter 3. ROSE

Rose, having average looks and a sharp mind, walked into the café confidently and plunked her designer handbag on the table in front of me. Rose worked several years as an assistant state attorney, prosecuting minor felonies and misdemeanors. She wanted to prosecute major felonies and longed to prosecute a murder or armed robbery case.

When top prosecuting state attorneys were head-hunted by large private law firms looking for good trial lawyers, vacancies were left in the State Attorney's office. Rose hoped she would be promoted, but for unknown reasons, she was continually passed over.

Her daily prosecution of third degree felonies meant she was continually negotiating with defense lawyers on relatively minor offenses. She did occasional short trials. She had a slightly below average record of wins and losses. She was a frustrated person and explained all this to me over a coffee on our first date.

I didn't care about her win - loss record. I hoped she would someday advance and prosecute major felonies. I paid more attention to her bright, glistening green eyes, focusing on me like a cat ready to pounce if I gave her the wrong look as she told me about herself.

I liked her and found I couldn't give her a wrong look. She kept a slight smile on her face as she told me her story and I liked that very much. Kind of a friendly, but still intimidating in a sexy and dangerous way. She dressed very well and her hair was, as they say, "Perfect".

We continued to date. As she told me more stories about the people she prosecuted for minor drug possessions and driving while intoxicated, I couldn't help interrupt her with comments as I wanted her to know I was listening to her long dialogs. Sluffing off my comments, she gave me the feeling she had "Know it all" tendencies and was bound and determined to have the last word, which occasionally led us into aimless talk -

"Wow, so the defendant you prosecuted passed the breathalyzer test yet he was still arrested for drunk driving?" I asked.

"Yes, a breathalyzer is just one indication of driving while intoxicated. The Officer had other indications."

"Like what?"

"His eyes could be blood shot, or his speech could be slurred, or signs of incoordination - like being unable to touch your nose with your arms stretched out, smell of alcohol, lots of factors." She said.

"What did the defendant who passed the breath test do?"

"Well, I can talk a little about this case since I'm limiting it to matters which are of public record. When the officer approached the car, the man was unresponsive and just kept looking forward and ignored the Officer's requests for his driver's license and registration. The Officer then opened the car door, and the driver started to get out but drunkenly tumbled out on the street." She laughed.

"Oh, so the driver staggers to his feet and takes a Breathalyzer and passes?" I said.

"Some people can drink a lot of alcohol and still be under the blood alcohol limit."

"You seem to be contradicting yourself? If legally, this person's blood alcohol level is below the limit, they aren't supposed to be legally drunk? Maybe the driver was sick or under drug influence?"

"Not in this case, he smelled of alcohol, his eyes were bright red like the sun rising in the morning sky, slurred speech, etc. Oh, he was drunk."

"Did a jury find him guilty?"

"No jury in this case. The judge decided it."

"So, you did your job and the judge ruled in your favor."

"Yes, we were very happy with the conviction."

"Have you ever convicted someone you thought might be innocent?"

"No."

"C'mon, Rose. I won't tell anyone."

"Nope, not me. I don't convict. I just present evidence."

"But have you ever felt someone might be innocent even though the evidence makes them guilty?"

"Not for me to decide. It's usually up to the judge or jury."

"But you want to win? Right?"

"Nope, not up to me."

"I see." I said. I thought I was beginning to beat the subject to death. So, I changed the subject.

"So, were you an egghead in law school? A girl in the top 10%?"

"If I thought there was a miscarriage of justice, I would bring it to the attention of the court." She said with green eyes blazing.

"Yes, I understand, - so, how did you do in law school?"

"I really would call it to the judge's attention."

"I know you would." I said.

"There may be innocent people in jail. We're just humans. We do the best we can."

"Okay, but why do I get the feeling you might have put some innocent people in jail?" I quietly asked her.

"Look, I haven't ever done that."

"Okay, sorry."

"I haven't and I am right and you are wrong to think that."

"I believe you."

"Nope, never did that."

We continued talking but she went on and on about not putting any innocent people in jail. She swore she wouldn't ever do that. We got up and I went to pay the check and she stepped in front of me and said

"I'll get this."

"No, I'll pay." I said.

"It's on me." She answered.

"Are you sure? There's not many girls who pay on the first date."

"I'm sure." She said.

"Well, thank you, Rose."

"Thank you."

I smiled at her.

"No problem."

Someone told me that if a person wants to have the last word it's not so much they want to prove anything, it's more the fact they want to make themselves feel better. So, I just simply said.

"Thank you again for the coffee, Rose. It was very nice meeting you."

"Nice meeting you too."

"Do you want to see me again?" I said.

"Do you want to see me again?"

"Yeah, we should meet again." I said.

"We should."

"Okay, I'll call you." I said.

"I'll call you."

Rose walked away and left me wondering about her. I hadn't given her my phone number and I didn't have her number either.

Dee's comments on Rose:

I think you might have had a rather lucky escape on this one, Bruce. I think you already had Rose's number and you were never going to win any argument in the future.

"Shall we go to bed now, dear?"

"Why? Are you bored with my company?"

No! I just thought you looked tired."

"Oh, so you're saying I don't look attractive?"

"That wasn't what I said! I think you look very attractive. So attractive, in fact, I'd like to take you to bed."

"Sex, sex, sex. That's all you think of. You don't even consider I might have had a long, hard, day. All I want is a good night's sleep, but no...."

You can see where this is going, can't you?

- Dee

"Everybody talks about the weather, but nobody ever does anything about it."
- Charles Dudley Warner

Chapter 4. JONATHAN

My planned meeting with Jonathan was not my finest hour. I had corresponded with Jonathan after he had contacted me on an Internet dating site, and this was our first meeting. He was late, and I didn't know what he looked like – I'd seen a photo, but it was a distance shot which he'd admitted was four years old, and he told me his hair had turned grey since it was taken.

It was pouring with rain and I was standing in the doorway of the bar near the waterfront where we had agreed to meet. I noticed a guy standing at the other end of the building, looking around, and then he started to walk towards me. I assumed he was the man I was supposed to meet.

I thought "Damn, he's not much to look at, and he's got a pot tummy." He came up to me and said hello.

"Hello, you must be Jonathan."

"Yes" he replied and we shook hands.

"Did you have any trouble finding the place?" I asked.

"No", he said. "I'm waiting for a boat."

I wondered what on earth he was talking about. Was our date to be on a boat? It was hosing, absolutely hosing down with rain.

"Are you a stranger in town?" I joked.

"No, I'm an inmate."

"Oh, you live here then? Why have you decided to take a cruise on a day like this, when you can't see a thing?"

I was beginning to realize this wasn't the man I was expecting to meet.

"I'm taking my company on an end of year cruise."

Oddly, he suddenly seemed several inches taller, five years younger, and there was no sign of the pot.

"I left my car at home in Remmers" (a very upmarket suburb of the city – another five years fell away) "so I don't know how I'm going to get home."

"You'll think of something" I responded.

"Yes, I guess I've got two or three hours to figure it out." (Perhaps he hadn't heard of taxis).

"So you're not Jonathan then?" (This girl is quick!)

"No." (What the hell did he think I'd asked him in the first place?") "So don't you know what your … um, acquaintance looks like?" he enquired.

"Well, I know he's about 5' 10." I blushed.

"That's right then" he said "give or take half an inch."

At this stage, there was nothing else to do but to bid each other a fond farewell and I was left falling about laughing, waiting for the real guy to turn up.

I could see Internet dating wasn't going to be boring!

Bruce's Comments on Jonathan:

My dear Dee,

My condolences to you for missing this fish.

Most women know when an eligible man tells you he doesn't have a ride home, you must drive him home. I realize hindsight is 20/20, but if you had had the presence of mind to offer to drive him home, he would have thanked you when you arrived at his home. He would then invite you in for a coffee or a wine, etc. etc., and you would have caught this fish.

Even if Jonathan refused your initial offer to drive him home, you could have insisted on giving him a ride and ignored his polite refusals. Just said "Stay put" then got your car and driven back to where he's waiting and forced him in your car if you had to.

Even better if your clothes were soaked from the rain! He would have had you take off all your clothes at his home and had them dried out – and that takes at least an hour. He'd have given you an expensive robe to wear while you sipped a wine with him and listened to music on his expensive home sound system. It doesn't get any more romantic than that on a first meet!

An added tip: Since Jonathan is a very interesting man, you should have offered to drive him home even if you didn't have your car with you. Just tell him to stay put and you will get your car and then rent a car if you must. And when you are driving him home, be sure to ask him about his company and compliment him on his business acumen. Even if he manufactures enema bags or cow manure, tell him he's a genius. In the latter case, ask him how a lactating cow produces 150 pounds of manure daily and compliment him on his management of all that.

The worst part of this kind of accidental meet-up is that it usually will not ever happen again. Even if you hung out at the dock where you met him, pretending to take photos or feeding seagulls and wearing a bikini, you probably will never run into him again.

Better luck next time!

-Bruce

"Do you smell it?
That smell…a kind of smelly smell.
The smelly smell that…smells."
-SpongeBob

Chapter 5. NOREEN

Noreen's profile revealed she had done many different things in her life. She graduated law school, but instead of taking the bar exam, she decided to start a retail shop selling women's clothing. She ran her store for several years. After that, she taught high school math for several years. Then she inherited her mother's estate and traveled for two years. She never had children. She was now looking for a serious relationship.

We met for a coffee and got along well. We talked for two hours straight and decided to continue to see each other. After a few dates, she asked me if I liked East Indian food

(I did) so she asked me over for dinner, telling me she loved to cook Indian dishes and even made her own curry from ingredients grown in her garden.

She had a very nice home not far from me and I marveled at her extensive landscaping and garden areas as I walked through her gate. All her beautiful trees, eight-foot hedges, plants and shrubs were symmetrically trimmed and it looked like her glorious property had just been featured in a landscaping magazine.

I walked up her front steps. On each side of the steps, and just behind the railings were large white trestles with white flowering vines. As I got to her door carrying my bottle of wine, I heard loud Indian music playing. I rang her doorbell. She was home but the loud music apparently was drowning out the sound of the doorbell. So, I knocked on door as loud as I could. No response. I continued to knock. She still didn't hear me.

I walked to the back of her house and walked up the stairs of her back porch. I was greeted with a strong smell of curry. More flowering plants revealed themselves as I ascended the back stairs. I looked through the window and there she was in front of the stove top covered with pots and pans, dancing away to the loud music. She had a large soup spoon in one hand, karaoking away to a song I hadn't ever heard. I tapped on her window with my car keys. She turned around and smiled.

She opened the back door and greeted me. She was wearing a white and pink apron with the words, "Pap-pee the Cook" (East Indian for "Kiss the Cook"). I tried to say something but she couldn't hear me over the loud music. I walked over to the stereo and turned it down.

"Okay to turn down your beautiful music?" I shouted.

"Oh, sorry, I get carried away sometimes." She laughed.

"So you've got a very real Indian theme tonight. This is way beyond cooking an Indian dish, and a very original and a new home visit experience for me." I said.

"My best girlfriend is Indian. You're going to meet her sometime. She's gorgeous.

Absolutely beautiful, mysterious and lots of fun. She got me interested in all this and I love it."

"Hey, I love your landscaping. One of the best yards I've ever seen."

"Oh, I love to garden especially in the summer. I walk around the yard, planting, trimming, getting tan, breathing fresh air... I'm one with nature... it's lovely to relax and enjoy my yard."

Noreen had a great figure for a petite lady -- probably a size 4 – with very wide hips and great legs bordering on "track and field legs" which were a bit over muscled for a woman, but very attractive.

I had to ask, "So what do you wear when you garden."

"My bikini! What else?" She laughed.

"I'll bet you stop traffic when you do the front of your yard?"

"Oh, it's great! I love to get a honk or a whistle now and then. I totally ignore it but it's great for the ego."

As we sat down for dinner, I was happy to see cutlery on the table as, I'd heard it's customary to eat Indian food with your fingers, something I hadn't ever done. She served dinner all at once and I watched her eat with her fingers, but didn't say a word.

Our conversation continued and she told me more about her Indian girlfriend and how much fun they have together.

"We just get crazy when we're together and can't help but act any other way. I've learned so much about the Indian culture, fashions, food, Tantric sex, etc."

"Oh, you like Tantric sex?" I asked.

"Tantric sex? Oh, I love it."

Noreen was 10 years younger than me. This was getting good, I thought. After dinner, we sat in her entertainment room having a strange liquor drink (which she said was called, Feni, which came from Goa, India) with soft Indian music playing. Out of the blue, she jumped up.

"I'm going to show you the eight basic Tantra sexual positions." She said.

"Fantastic!" I said and started to unbutton my shirt.

"Keep your clothes on!" She said, as she plopped herself down on my lap.

We started laughing and I was getting hooked on this fun woman and very horny at the same time. As she twisted and turned herself into various sexual positions with me, I couldn't help but notice for the first time, her strong body odor. She didn't use deodorant. I got a big whiff of her as she was moving around but we were having so much fun teasing each other, I didn't say anything.

Then I kissed her thinking I would give her my best romantic kiss on her lips but instead got a full, wet, saliva-dripping wide open mouth kiss. I started to pull back but she followed me and put her tongue down my throat.

Wow! I thought. I hadn't ever felt a tongue like that. Amazing woman, but even though I was still turned on, her odor began to turn me off.

She nodded to me with her head motioning me to the bedroom. I cooled down some as I went through her bedroom door. Even though we made love, her odor got stronger and eventually made me feel ill and her feet were dirty.

When I went home the next day, I couldn't get the smell out of my nostrils even though I brushed the inside of my nose with my toothbrush. I wasn't sure how to mention it without hurting her feelings.

On our next date, she got in my car and after talking a bit, I decided to ask.

"You don't use deodorant?" I asked.

"Oh, you noticed? Do I smell?"

"No. But I sensed you like the Indian culture and isn't it common not to use deodorant in India?"

"There's just a lot of harmful chemicals in it. I don't notice a difference and feel better without it. You should throw away your deodorant and try it." She said.

I smiled but didn't want to say anything. We stayed in touch, but went our separate ways. She's found a younger man and things are going well for her.

Dee's comments on Noreen:

When Noreen asked "Do I smell?" You said no? Why? Why? Why?

This was your chance to do a great service for all mankind, but you missed your chance. Noreen's new man obviously lacked any sense of smell, lucky guy, and so, it appears, did she.

You could, perhaps, have suggested making love in Noreen's stunning garden. All that manure and fertilizer would hide a multitude of olfactory problems. And just think! A little Tantric sex with a gardenia up your bottom would give new meaning to "sensational sex!"

-Dee

*"We do not remember days, we
remember moments."*
- Cesare Pavese

Chapter 6. THE REAL JONATHAN

Jonathan, the guy I'd planned to meet at
the waterfront bar, did turn up a short time
later. My first impression was that I wasn't
sure he was worth the wait. He was dressed
in a white collared t-shirt, green pants and a
navy bomber jacket, and was in rather a foul
temper. It appeared he'd mistaken where we
were to meet and had been waiting at the
wrong bar. He's finally checked his phone
and established where he was supposed to
be, but his tone as he related this implied it
was somehow my fault

Jonathan eventually settled down and
his manner became more pleasant. We talked
about our backgrounds and he told me he had

never been married, nor had any children. He'd been sent to boarding school from the age of seven, and he talked about how hard it had been at prep school and how this had resulted in low self-esteem. Jonathan said he had found it very hard to ask women for dates when he was younger, even though he realized now he'd been extremely eligible, as the family was very well off. He was now in real estate and property.

"The only way to make money out of property is to never sell." Jonathan advised.

Jonathan spoke of his longest relationship. "She was beautiful, but she was a spinner."

"In what way?" I wondered.

"Oh, she screamed at me every time I went out, because she reckoned I was with other women."

"And were you?"

"Well, I guess I often was" he admitted.

We were together for an hour and a half, although Jonathan didn't seem to be listening to me all that closely. He had a handwritten list from my profile, which I thought was a bit comical, and I laughed at him as he referred to it. He said it was to remind him of the things he wanted to ask, and I was happy to answer his questions. Whatever was on his checklist, I appeared to pass, and Jonathan invited me to dinner the following Saturday.

I felt I should give Jonathan the benefit of the doubt over the impression he'd first given me, thinking perhaps he'd been nervous, and hadn't handled it well. His confession, however, about being unfaithful didn't give me confidence in his potential as a possible partner.

Our second date was more pleasant, and Jonathan seemed now very keen. At the end of the evening, he offered to drive me to my car, which was parked a little way away. We drove there and he parked the car, and leaned in for a kiss. He was a good kisser, but eventually became so ardent my lips began to hurt from his 5 o'clock shadow.

I broke away to say goodbye and thank him for the evening. Jonathan did not take this well. An angry expression crossed his face, and I hastily got out of his vehicle and closed the door. As I walked over to my car, I heard Jonathan throw his BMW into a mad turn, with a squeal of tires, and I could hear the wheels spin as his car roared away at high speed.

With a temper so volatile, I concluded this was a path I didn't want to take, so didn't respond to his later messages.

Bruce's comments on the Real Jonathan:

I'm glad you got away from this one, unless you like racing cars?

When you first met him, he seemed to blame you for not being able to read his mind, or, in the very least, know in advance that he would choose the wrong bar. I know men do this; and I know women never do this.

I once heard an almost unbelievable story about a man who foolishly asked an annoyed woman, "What's wrong?"

And her response, believe it or not, was a cold stare then "Don't you know?"

The man got smart and said nothing. But you well know what she said next which was, "You should know..."

Can you, in your wildest imaginings, believe a woman actually expects a man to be a telepath and read her mind? Am I misunderstanding this?

If you really desired Jonathan "Number 2" (pun intended), you should have yelled out when he screeched away, "Oh, you want to race?"

Then run to your car and peeled out after him, making sure you were in his rear-view mirror, smiling adventurously at him while the wind was blowing your blouse half open and wildly splaying your blonde hair.

He would have been very hot for you! And, you could have taught him how to shave and kiss too!

- Bruce

"The road to excess leads to the palace of wisdom…for we never know what is enough until we know what is more than enough."
-William Blake

Chapter 8. BERNICE

After mutually ending a brief relationship with a woman who was more interested in my assets than in me, I was playing golf with some friends of mine and we talked about gold diggers.

One of my friends suggested, "Hey, I don't care what she's after, as long as she's great looking with a great body. Beautiful women know this. If you're able to afford them they will treat you like a king."

"Yeah, but I want a woman who actually likes me." I said.

Men love a beautiful sexy woman and our emotions run deep during great sex which makes the relationship stronger. But for a guy like me, wanting a life partner again, I know sex with a gorgeous woman is wonderful, but it eventually wears off. Sex, in my view, is better with a woman you truly love, and who loves you. You must make sure you truly love the woman you wake up with each morning. You may have heard the often-repeated quote, "Show me the most beautiful woman in the world and I'll show you a man who's tired of bonking her."

Another guy in our foursome suggested I give "Bernice" a call.

"Bern's a young widow, and not a gold digger."

I had seen Bernice. She was attractive, athletic, intelligent and a low golf handicapper.

After finishing the round and a couple of drinks afterwards, I started out the door when I noticed other friends of mine I hadn't seen in a while, so I walked over and sat down at their table to say hello. These guys were older golfers who had been members of the club for many years and knew most everyone. I asked them if they knew Bernice.

The older guys were known to not say anything bad about anyone in the Club. It was their strict policy to keep quiet if they had nothing positive to say about another member.

As I sat down with them, one of the old guys asked me if I had found anyone and I mentioned I was thinking of giving Bernice a call. His face and the rest of their faces went sour giving me a discouraging look. I sat there puzzled.

Then, another old guy said, "She's nice," and another said, "She's a good golfer," and then another said, "I knew her late husband very well and he was a great guy."

The guy who mentioned her late husband was fighting with himself to keep quiet. After a long pause, he continued, "I know Bern very well, and did you know Bruce…she's been widowed twice?"

Okay. That's interesting, I thought. I started to ask about her further but the old guys changed the subject and began talking about something else. Left hanging, I exited and called Bernice to ask her out.

"Yes, I'd love to go out with you Bruce. We should have a game together, say, Saturday?"

"That's a date Bernice, I'll get a tee time and we'll just play by ourselves. I heard some nice things about you and want to get to know more." I said.

"Call me 'Bern'. Who told you about me?"

"Just asked around at the Club, and everyone was complimentary. Ah, let's have a lunch after our round. Okay?"

Bern beat me by five strokes on Saturday. After the round, we had lunch.

"I heard your last husband was a great guy." I said. Bern looked down and I could see tears starting. "Oh sorry, I didn't mean to...."

"No that's alright... Heart attack. He was gone too quick. It was very short."

"Well I'm glad you're getting over it." I said, trying to be consoling.

"Yes, I've been through this before one other time. My other husband had a bad heart too."

I didn't want to ask any further. I wondered about her and she was a very good looking woman.

"Are you going to the Club dinner next Saturday night?" She asked.

"I heard about it but I'm not dating anyone, so do you want to go together?"

She gave me a big smile and said, "That would be nice!"

Saturday evening came around and I picked her up. As we walked in to the Dining Room, we saw members and their spouses mingling and having drinks before dinner. Bern had been a member of the Club a lot longer than I and knew most everyone. I watched her eyes scan the room. Then she focused on a group and turned to me and said, "I'll be back."

I stood there and watched her walk over to two guys who welcomed her with hugs and kisses. I went over to the bar. One of the older members I had talked to before about Bernice was standing there with a big smirk on his face having just watched our entrance. I tried to act like all was normal. His smirk turned into a chuckle.

"I know you guys don't say bad things about other members, but what the hell?" I said.

He started to give me a let's calm down look. Then shook his head and said,

"You will see. She's a great lady. She's buried two of them so far. We tried to warn you."

"Warn me about what?" I asked.

"Oh, you'll find out." He walked away.

I stood at the bar and ordered a beer for myself. Bern already had a glass of champagne in her hand, and was talking away with two men. They were laughing, touching and poking each other, all having a great time while I was Mr. Stupid at the bar.

I sat down alone at the table with people I didn't know waiting for Bern to join me. When the salad began to be served, Bern came over and sat down next to me.

"I'm so sorry, I hadn't seen those guys in years."

"That's okay. Where are their wives?"

"Oh, they're both single but have girlfriends." Bern then got up and scanned the dining room, then turned to me and said, "Wait...."

She got up and went over to their table on the other side of the large dining room and sat down with the two guys she's been talking to before. I sat alone eating dinner making small talk with the other members at our table.

After dinner, there was a small dance band playing and I watched couples dance as I stood alone at the bar talking to Fred, the bartender. I finished my drink and began to leave when out of the corner of my eye I saw Bernice walking fast toward me.

"Hey, I'm awfully sorry. This was totally unexpected. I'll make it up to you."

"That's okay Bern. Hell, you haven't seen those guys in years. I understand." I left.

About a month later, I played golf with another guy I know at the Club whose wife was one of Bern's best friends.

"You still looking for a girl?" He asked me.

"Well, I dated a few but nothing serious."

"Look, Bern is really sorry for leaving you at the dinner. Hell, you got to give her another chance. She likes you. She's got plenty of money so there's no strain on you, and hell, she's a great cook, loves golf, loves life and she'll have sex all day with you."

"George...did your wife put you up to this?" I asked.

"Bern is a great lady and she's been through a lot. She was very close to one of those guys at the Club dinner but that's not going anywhere. She wants you. You won't be disappointed."

As George said that, reminder images of the faces of the old golfers all having discouraging looks appeared over George's shoulder.

"Okay, I'll take her to one more dinner. I think she'd make a great partner but if I'm not the one for her, I'm sure she'll find someone." I said.

I took Bern out dinner and we had a quiet, friendly dinner and a good time. She was interesting to talk to and fun to be with. Full of life and adventure. I took her home and she asked me in for a nightcap and before I knew it we were in bed making love. She seemed as though she couldn't get enough. We changed positions every few minutes. Up, down, and around, she was having her way with me. I tried to dominate, but we would roll together several times, each of us trying to get on top. Finally, I fell off the bed. She jumped down on me. It lasted most of the night and after a short nap, she woke me early to make love again.

It brought back memories from my teen years. My back and other muscles ached for a few days afterwards.

We continued to date but our feelings for each other gradually wore off and we drifted apart. She is a fun lady and we are still friends today.

Dee's comments on Bernice:

No wonder the old boys were looking at you a little sideways, they knew Bernice was the better golfer and they felt uncomfortable, knowing you were going to lose every game, but not wanting to tell you.

The two previous husbands had obviously whacked away at their balls to no avail, Bernice was always going to beat them. And we all know men hate to lose. I bet if you'd enquired further, you'd have found they'd passed away on the green, desperately trying to sink their putts, or in a sand trap. And meantime, Bernice would have been arriving at the nineteenth hole, looking for another foursome to sign up with....

-Dee

"After all is said and done, sit down."
- Bill Copeland

Chapter 8. PAOLO

It was something of a comedy of errors the night I met Paolo, and this time it was all my fault. We'd arranged to meet at a trendy little place in the suburbs, but becoming somewhat jaded with online dating, I'd neglected to read his message properly and waited in the wrong place. I had his cell phone number, so I rang Paolo twice, but it went to voicemail. After 15 minutes, I gave up and went and sat in my car.

Meantime, Paolo was waiting in the right place, until he too eventually gave up and returned to his vehicle, where he found the messages from me on his phone, which he'd politely left in his car. We finally met up!

After ordering our glasses of wine, Paolo told me he'd recently lost his wife of many years to cancer. He was naturally wearing his wedding ring still, which he turned as he spoke.

"I should probably move my wedding ring to the other hand", he said, showing sensitivity.

I lay my hand on his to stop him doing so, and he smiled gratefully.

Paolo had the most beautiful brown eyes, which filled with tears as he spoke about his wife. He had the sexiest Italian accent. I felt I could listen to him for hours, even though he was speaking of another woman. Paolo told me about his life in Italy, and explained why they'd moved so far across the world, where they started a very successful company which he now ran alone. He talked too of his love of flying in his private plane, and of how his cares lessened when he was in the air.

Although I felt it was far too soon for him to be dating, as he'd obviously not allowed himself time to grieve, we arranged to meet again. This time we were the last people left in the restaurant. Paolo invited me back to his nearby home for coffee, where he played on both his grand piano and a guitar, and sang beautifully in Italian. He was very talented.

Paolo eventually laid the guitar aside, then took me in his arms and kissed and caressed me. After a few very enjoyable moments, much to my dissatisfaction, he pushed me gently away and said in his liquid accent "I'm so sorry, I know it's ridiculous, but I feel I'm being unfaithful."

Although we'd spoken during dinner about meeting again, it was just "goodbye" when I left about midnight, and I was devastatingly disappointed, but Paolo later rang and asked to meet again before he left on a business trip to Italy. Unfortunately, I wasn't able to make it.

Later, when I hadn't heard from him, I did phone him a couple of weeks after he was due back from Italy, and he responded that he was in the throes of packing his wife's possessions and that he would be in touch. I didn't, however, hear from Paolo again until nearly two years later, when he emailed to say he'd like to meet again.

To my surprise, when we met, it transpired that whilst I thought Paolo was pining for his wife, he was beginning a relationship with another woman, Barbara, which is why he hadn't contacted me again! Barbara had recently been killed by a drunken driver in a dreadful accident. Once again, Paolo wasn't giving himself time to grieve, and equally foolish, I allowed myself to be drawn in by his charm, and that adorable Italian accent.

We were together for about a year, but our relationship never really worked well. Paolo constantly talked about Barbara, even in moments of passion. I felt I was always being compared (though not unkindly) to her and other times to his wife, and it became infuriating. I just couldn't compete with the dear departed and eventually decided it was time to call it a day.

Paolo professed to be devastated by our breakup, but I knew, going by his past record, Paolo wasn't going to miss me for long.

Bruce's comments on Paolo:

Dear Dee,

There's not much I can say here. I love this story and the way you handled him.

I have a feeling he will be calling you back when he fully realizes your sensitivity and understanding.

-Bruce.

"How to gain success in life:
1. Be Asian.
2. Follow step 1."
- Anonymous

Chapter 9. ZHANG LI

In Chinese, the female name, "Zhang Li" means "Beautiful". She and I met on a blind date arranged by the Asian wife of a friend of mine named Tom.

I walked into the café and noticed her right away. She was sitting alone at a table just inside the door smiling at me. Very attractive about 5 feet 6 inches, 130 lbs, beautiful long dark hair, lovely dark eyes and a very warm smile, she looked like she just stepped out of a James Bond Movie. She resembled the beautiful villain "Ling", from the movie, "You Only Live Twice." Ling, a female villain, almost killed James if he hadn't pressed a button to flip up the bed against the wall with her in it. I dismissed my villain thoughts, realizing I hadn't dated an Asian woman before and she was breath taking. I was hooked and determined to date this woman.

I well knew superficial relationships based on looks alone don't last. I was enamored by her beauty. As she spoke to me, I didn't care what she was saying, I was infatuated with her. I kept reminding myself, I was looking for a soul-mate and told myself to focus on learning about Zhang Li, the person, her likes and dislikes, etc. Did I take my own advice? No way.

Our meeting went well since my dazed eyes were doing all the real talking and she was reeling me in. I wasn't sure where this potential relationship would take me, but I didn't care.

She asked me if I liked the Asian culture. I didn't know much about it, so I told her I always wanted to have dinner at a Chinese restaurant with a beautiful Chinese woman who would order dinner for both of us from an unreadable Chinese menu. I asked her out to dinner to see if she would do that and she agreed.

On our first dinner date, she picked the restaurant, "Mian" and we arrived in the early evening. An older Chinese couple were the only patrons there when we sat down. She ordered for us in Chinese. There was soft Chinese bamboo flute music playing.

I learned she was from Hong Kong where she worked for a Chinese TV shopping network like Home Shopping Network. She pitched products and was very successful at it. She asked me if I was interested in buying real estate.

"No, not really, my investments are in order and I don't want to disturb them."

"You mus' make monee." She replied staring me right in the eye. "You know Lemon Hill Apartments?" She asked in her strong Chinese accent.

"Yes, that's the new planned residential development near downtown. They're advertising pre-construction sales right now."

"I know the developer. He a friend of mine. He develop large apartments, shopping centers in Hong Kong. I bought 11 apartments."

Her mood changed from flirting to business in an instant. Taken aback somewhat, I instinctively slowed the conversation.

"So tell me how you got to know the developer in Hong Kong." I asked.

"We date for a while. Then when he came here to develop I follow him and I show you apartments. You want to see?"

"Oh, you mean walk through the models?"

"Yes, only need 10% down. Done in two years. Very good investment."

The last thing I wanted to do was to experiment with investments but I was still in a "Huang hu" – an ecstatic trance with her charm and persuasiveness.

"You pay bill now. I take you."

Pay bill? Like a cold, wet dishrag in the face, the words, "Pay bill" instantly snapped me out of my trance. I shook my head several times. I didn't know what to think since it was happening so fast but began to understand my wallet was of more interest to her than I was.

Yet, I was curious about her. She said she contracted to purchase 11 apartments but would assign them to buyers (flip them) for a profit prior to being required to close. She was seriously into real estate and lived in a very nice part of town, had an expensive car, and dressed very well. I fought with myself but began to understand she had no romantic interest in me. But even though I knew I was being reeled in, I had to see where this was going.

"Yeah, I might want to look at the models sometime. You never know when you might run into something good. I will go and look when I get a chance." I said.

"No, I must take you there. I know the developer. I get you discount."

Yeah right, I thought. She's looking for a finder's fee. Anyone selling real estate needs a license. I was a bit familiar with finder fees or referral fees that go to unlicensed persons as a practical way to help move real estate. She would probably walk through the models with me with a licensed agent of the developer. But I didn't want to go there yet.

I was losing interest in her since she changed so quickly from an incredibly charming woman to a very assertive real estate salesperson. Then again, if she personally knew the developer, perhaps I could get a discount? I wasn't sure what to believe. So, we made a date to have her take me there and meet the developer.

When we walked in to the preconstruction model apartment, the developer wasn't there. Instead we were greeted by a Chinese salesperson and Zhang Li spoke to her at length in Chinese.

After hearing them talk for five minutes, Zhang Li motioned me to wait while she and the salesperson went to a back office and in a few minutes the sales manager came out to greet me with Zhang Li. I learned all about the development, but there wasn't any mention of a discount as I was given a folder with the project's plans, details and prices.

I took the folder and opened it while the sales manager told me that Zhang Li and a salesperson would show the models. We walked through two models, and I didn't like the apartments since they were very small and might be problematic to rent even though they were in a good location close to the Central Business District.

"Zhang Li, where is this discount you told me about?" I asked.

"Oh, no worries. I take care of it. If you like, I will talk to him."

"Do you get money from the developer if I buy the apartment?"

"Not your business."

"Zhang Li, I like discounts, but I don't want to get involved if you don't have a license?"

"No! No! I am his friend. No worries."

I was turned off. She saw my face and started to flirt with her body language trying to hold my interest. But that was a turn off. This was all too quick. She drove me back to her place and I thanked her and left.

About five weeks later, Tom, the friend of mine whose wife arranged my initial meet with Zhang Li, called me up and invited me to Yum Cha with his wife and told me Zhang Li wanted to see me again. Great, I thought. She was a charmer and an interesting successful woman. Maybe she wants to get to know me more? Maybe I rushed too quickly on judging her? I told Tom I would meet them there.

When I walked into the crowded Chinese restaurant, Tom, his wife, Zhang Li and another much older man were seated at the table. What kind of game is this, I thought?

Zhang Li saw me come in and got up and approached me and told me she was glad I could come. She was paying for the Yum Cha and the older man had an interest in her developer friend's apartments, so she asked him to join us at the last moment. I scratched my head. I looked at Tom and his wife, who were both giving me a "come and sit down" look, so I did. There were friendly introductions.

The old guy turned to me and asked, "Zhang Li tells me you saw the new apartments?"

"Yes, very nice but I wasn't keen on going further." Zhang Li moved her chair away from me and closer to her buyer. She was continuing her sales routine coming out with guns blazing after I said that. I knew she was difficult to refuse. I was still broken up about my unwanted divorce and still spinning from my ex-wife's plotting and planning to get me out of our beautiful home and had great respect for the female scheming ability. But, hell, I thought. Relax. Nothing I can do here. So, I'll have some fun watching Zhang Li in action.

Zhang Li continued to work her magic on the old guy. She played with his jacket lapels, his collar, smiling ear-to-ear. She was going to take him on the apartment tour. I could tell the old guy was more interested in Zhang Li than the apartments.

My phone beeped. A text came in from a lady who I had met a few days ago asking me how I was. Her interest in me reminded me what I was looking for – someone interested in me as a person rather than an apartment buyer. I stayed the rest of the dinner and watched Zhang Li reel in this nice old guy.

I thought back to when Zhang Li showed me the models. She didn't sit on any of the beds, but I wondered if there was a button I could press to flip the bed up against the wall? I pictured pressing that button to flip the bed as she sat on the bed handing me a pen to sign a contract.

I came out of my Walter Mitty fantasy, and saw my friend and his wife also watching Zhang Li in action. They turned to me and nodding their sympathies and understanding of the commercial-romantic situation going on, silently apologizing. I nodded back telling them no problem. Hell, I thought. Zhang Li is trying to make a sale and she's using all she's got to get it done. I hoped she makes the sale with the old guy.

I left right after dinner. Zhang Li saw me get up out of the corner of her eye, then stood up to see me off and walked me out the door. I smiled and told her I hoped the old guy was interested in her friend's apartments and we each promised to stay in touch. She was an interesting woman.

Dee's comments on Zhang Li:

That button to flip the bed against the wall could come in very handy in a multitude of situations. Every home should have one.

I'm afraid Zhang Li was much more interested in making sales than making love, but you must respect her work ethic. Don't waste time making love when you could be making money.

I can see now where I was going wrong.

-Dee

*"I've been waiting for Prince Charming
like every other little girl."
- Shelly Burch*

Chapter 10. RYAN

Ryan was a flight steward, who I met when I was flying home for the holidays. He was amusing and fun, and we met up again and got on well together.

He rang one Wednesday evening, and we made a date for Friday night in the city. As the weekend neared, work became horrendously busy, and on the Friday, I wondered whether I was going to get away in time to get to our meeting. I raced home, showered so fast the water barely had time to hit, threw on clothes and makeup and dashed out.

It was a horrible night and the rain was so bad I could barely see the lane markings, and barely found my way by following the car tail-lights in front of me until we were in the city. I parked and raced to our meeting place, hoping I wasn't too drenched or too late. There was a waitress standing outside under the awning, holding a menu (as they do) and she was very concerned.

"Are you waiting for someone? Oh, is he late...?"

The place was crowded and right up against the window was a table of women I knew, all busily waving at me (while I tried to ignore them!) Finally, I thought I'd better go inside to see if my date was in there, so in I went and sat with them for a few minutes. They all commiserated.

"Oh, is he late?"

"Hasn't he rung you?"

"That's why I don't date, I couldn't handle it" .... etc, etc.

I tried to tell them I wasn't too concerned, I was confident something must have happened, he was too keen to have stood me up. There were lots of knowing glances at each other and pitying looks at me.

"Stood up!" one lady mouths to her friend, nodding wisely, as she returned with a drink. She realized I was watching her, reflected in the window, and donned an innocent look.

I ventured outside again only to get another waitress "Are you waiting for someone? Is he late? Oh, that's too bad."

I gave Ryan 35 minutes in case there'd been some confusion about the time, then gave up and went home, picking up a hamburger on the way.

My son was at home, and he was upset on my behalf, smarting at my humiliation.

"You should ring him, Mom, and blast him for standing you up! That's just not right."

Eventually, after I'd finished my hamburger, I did pick up the phone to ring – only to hear the 'message waiting' beep. Sure enough, it was Ryan. He'd left a message at 1.30pm to say he had food poisoning from his meal the night before, and to please ring him because he wasn't able to go anywhere, he'd be home all night! If only I'd checked my messages! But I'd been in such a hurry, and no-one ever leaves messages on the home phone, they always text. Oh, but I forgot, he lived in an area that doesn't have cell phone reception....

Ryan and I did date for a while, he was a nice guy, but there wasn't the right chemistry between us, and sadly our dating eventually faded away.

Bruce's comments on Ryan:

My dear Dee,

Ryan might have been putting you on? Food poisoning? Yeah, right.

While I was in college, there was a jock that made three dates for Saturday night. Then he'd decide which girl he would want to take out on a date on Friday and call the other two girls and give them an excuse. The jock didn't give simple excuses. He said the girls wouldn't believe simple excuses, and he might want to take them out later. So, his excuses went like this:

"I'm very sorry, but I must cancel tomorrow night because:

1. My sister just had a miscarriage. It was her first one. My brother in law is out of town, and I'm going over to help her through it this weekend."

2. I'm in Key West and I got four flat tires. I was trying to catch a guy who raced away in his car after snatching an old woman's purse and knocking her down. Had to do some wild driving but I got him arrested

after chasing him for miles all over creation. The lady got her purse back. The gas station says I have to wait until Monday to get the tires."

3. I'm at the Mayo Clinic in Hastings, Minnesota. I was getting dizzy spells and the doctors aren't sure what's going on with me. My parents had me flown out here. They're at least keeping me here till Monday or Tuesday. And so on... He was imaginative.

Finally, I wish I was there when one of your friends mouthed "Stood up" in front of you. I would have grabbed some flowers off a table and approached you with flowers in hand saying, "Hi Dee! I was here waiting in the back of this crowded restaurant looking for you constantly. I glanced at this table several times but didn't think you would be at this table with these large older ladies sitting by themselves, not having dates tonight."

I'd say that last part while directly looking at the lady who mouthed "Stood up."

How's that for an excuse?

-Bruce

"There comes a time, when you walk away from the drama and the people who create it. Better to surround yourself with people who make you laugh and forget the bad, and focus on the good. Stay and appreciate people who treat you right. Life is too short to be anything but happy. Falling down is part of life, getting back up is living and a hard fall means a high bounce if you're made of the right material."

-Anonymous

Chapter 11. MARCIA

Something about Marcia's face attracted me. She looked very independent and strong. I asked her to meet me over a glass of wine. She agreed and we hit it off very well and agreed to continue to date.

Our dating continued each weekend after our first meet-up. I had the feeling my search was over. She asked me to spend a weekend with her at her Wisconsin vacation cottage. This was going to be our first overnight and I was happy things were progressing.

Marcia told me on our first meet she was out of prison about a year. She had a boyfriend who sold drugs and without going into details she was arrested with him and convicted. I hadn't dated an ex-convict before, and I felt sorry for her and wanted to give her a chance to be treated normally. Her account of her arrest and conviction seemed like she was just in the wrong place at the wrong time. She pleaded guilty and cooperated with police and did some time.

Trying to start a new life, she enrolled in an accounting program at a junior college and was much older than her young classmates. She was determined to work hard to make a new life. She was intelligent and attractive and although when I heard she'd been in prison, I was thinking of leaving, after talking with her, I liked her and asked her out.

Her Wisconsin cottage was a small one bedroom cabin on seven acres in the middle of the forest off a main road. The stars came out so big at night you could almost reach out and touch them. Her father had passed away and left it to her. We walked the property and she pointed out trees her father planted on the property and how proud she was of the place.

After I barbequed dinner for us, we spent the evening talking and drinking wine and I loved it and was happy I had dated her. Marcia asked me if I wanted to go to bed around 9:30pm. There wasn't anything I would rather do.

She lit a few candles around the room and I put my arms around her and we made love. I was at peace with this woman and loved to be with her.

After we finished our lovemaking, I lay on my back and we talked quietly. Then I stretched my right arm and put my hand under her pillow and felt something foreign. I remembered feeling an object under her pillow during our lovemaking, but didn't bother about it. I put my hand under her pillow again, and pulled out a butcher knife.

"Marcia, do you know you have a butcher's knife under your pillow?"

She didn't say anything, but took the knife from me and put it on the table.

"I come up here alone and when you're a single girl you can't be too careful."

"I understand. Has anyone ever tried to break in while you were here?"

"Once, a friend of my old boyfriend came by and left after I told him I'd call the police if he didn't leave."

We dozed off but we were awoken by the sound of a motorcycle coming up her driveway.

"Stay here." She told me.

"Wait." I said.

"If he sees you…there's trouble."

"Oh… there will be blood?" I mumbled to myself as she went downstairs in her robe. The motorcycle engine noise stopped and I heard the kickstand click down. Then footsteps to the door.

Some horny past friend of boyfriend drug guy is coming here sniffing around, I thought.

I heard talking then heard her yell, "I'm calling the police."

I heard a male voice saying something, then the door slammed. Heard more footsteps outside and the motorcycle engine start up, then roar and fade away. Then heard nothing. I got out of bed. Then heard her coming up the stairs.

"Damn." She said.

"You got rid of him fast. You calling the police?"

"I might if he comes back. But, he won't."

"What makes you so sure he won't come back?" I said.

"If he's arrested for trespass, he'll go back to jail."

I felt very sad her life was complicated somewhat by her past. I hoped she eventually found some peace but I decided to move on.

Dee's comments on Marcia:

Hmm. It's hard to find any comment to make here, Bruce. I've found in the past a butcher's knife just tends to cast a real damper on any romantic moments.

Add in a jailbird boyfriend on a motorbike, and passion just seems to fly right out the window, for some unknown reason.

-Dee

"Love is a smoke made with the fume of sighs."
- William Shakespeare

Chapter 12. TOM

It had been a lovely, sunny day, but a gusty breeze had risen. As I waited for Tom I was beginning to wish I'd worn a jacket over my light, summery dress. Tom and I had met when we worked for neighboring companies, and when he'd heard I was leaving my job, he'd suggested we should catch up for a meal as he didn't want to lose touch. I was happy to do so, as I thought Tom was an attractive, personable man, being around 6' tall, and quite nice looking. He held a senior management position in the company he worked for, so his intelligence was also appealing. I felt there was definitely some chemistry between us and I'd been looking forward to this, our first date.

I was delighted when Tom arrived, he was only a few minutes late, which I didn't mind as I always tend to arrive early for meetings or appointments. He gave me a warm hug, and kissed me in greeting.

We went for a drink in a nearby bar, which was lovely, and I started to warm up from my chilly wait. After a drink or two, Tom asked if I'd like to go for a meal, and suggested a nearby restaurant.

"Oh, great,' I responded "that sounds lovely".

As we left the bar, I was glad the restaurant was nearby, as by now the evening was becoming even cooler.

"Wait!" Tom said, and he seemed to be shuffling through his wallet. "I had a coupon. I must have left it in the car."

"A coupon?"

"Yes. We can get 25% off whatever we order. Would you mind if we walked back to the car to get it?"

Ohh-kay. It seemed important to him, so of course I agreed, and off we went. Or rather, off he went and off I tottered. It never seems to occur to men that when we women dress up for a date, we don't always have practicalities in mind, and on this occasion my 4" high heels and flimsy dress were not designed for a long hike. I would have been better off wearing Sherpa gear and tramping boots, because Tom's car was parked at what seemed miles away from our meeting point.

Tom explained he resented paying parking charges, and therefore always parked in suburban street parks where he didn't have to pay. By the time we found his car and the rotten coupon, and made our way back to the restaurant, I was turning blue and felt as though I had bowed legs and blisters.

The meal was very pleasant, however, and although I found Tom's conversational skills a little dull, I liked him enough to agree to a second date the following weekend. We agreed on a movie we both wanted to see.

Having learned my lesson, this time I dressed a little warmer and wore flat shoes, just in case, but it really wasn't necessary.

We met and headed for the ticket office, and Tom and I lined up in the queue. To the surprise of both myself and the cashier, however, Tom was convinced that there was a 'two for the price of one' deal running at the theatre, and it took quite some time for him to be convinced that this wasn't so. Of course, to ease his disappointment, I offered to pay, but Tom was a kind man and wouldn't accept. He finally paid for the two tickets, and the long queue that had gathered behind us started again to move.

The film began and I for one became engrossed in the story. Tom took my hand, which I thought was sweet, and he began to caress my arm. The film was a gripping thriller, and I was on the edge of my seat. Then I became distracted as I realized Tom was still stroking my arm, over, and over, and over again, until I began to feel he was wearing a rut. I completely lost my focus on the movie, as I wondered how to shake him off without offending him. I tried leaning further away, but this didn't stop the stroking, so I leaned a little closer, hoping he would at least move to a different spot on my arm or even better, stop altogether, but no, instead the stroking simply became a little more frantic, still in the same rut, until I feared he was about to draw blood! Thank God, the movie finally came to an end, though I have no idea whether the heroine had survived, as by now I was plotting a murder of my own.

I did eventually see the funny side, and Tom and I ended up dating for a while, until my new job took me to another city and we eventually lost touch.

Bruce's comments on Tom:

Haha! I see you are quoting Shakespeare's Romeo and Juliet about how the pains of love brings tears to your eyes the way smoke makes your eyes tear? So, now you are saying, "Rubbing my arm in the same place 2000 times creates friction and the smoke emanating from my arm is bringing tears to my eyes?" Very classy, Dee! Tom didn't realize rubbing two sticks together won't start a fire in your heart.

I like Tom. He was just nervous. He's a practical man and you broke his heart. I think you would have tried to remain friends with him if he wasn't so persistent?

Friends are good to have. You might need coins for a parking meter with a meter maid standing over you to write you one. If Tom passed you with a pocketful of change, do you think he would offer to help get you out of the ticket? Especially, if you were still in the same city, not having moved to another city?

- Bruce

"Sex without love is a meaningless
experience, but as far as meaningless
expressions go it's pretty damn good."
-Woody Allen

Chapter 13. CHRISTA

My curiosity was aroused when I read
Christa's profile. She was born in Ireland, a
place and culture I hadn't yet experienced.
We messaged back and forth several times
and then arranged to meet at a café about
midway between our homes.

I watched her walk into the café. She
smiled as she approached me with her 5'6"
large boned frame, large green eyes and
auburn hair and a meek and graceful walk.
She was dressed in a long sleeved white
blouse buttoned to the neck, with a vintage
style flowered knee length skirt hiding a very
curvaceous figure.

I stood and pulled out a chair for her. I sat down and watched her for an instant, then thanked her for meeting me. I gave her a brief history of myself and she told me about her story. She grew up in Cork County on a farm.

I enjoyed listening to her Irish accent. She enjoyed living in the US and loved Disney World and had just come out of a relationship. She reminded me of a wholesome kindergarten teacher - very unassuming and open - someone you would be proud to be with and someone you wouldn't hesitate to bring home to meet your parents. I asked her to dinner and she agreed.

I picked Christa up outside her home and over dinner I got a chance to get to know more about her. We ate a light meal and talked continuously for two hours.

Her relationship with her past boyfriend went sour and it seemed from what she said they grew tired of each other. She was a quiet person, who didn't play sports. She would cycle a bit, go for long walks and liked to read.

She worked in an office for an insurance company and her social life centered around her sister "Alannah" and her brother-in-law and their friends.

At dinner, she wore a dark blue high neck laced dress with half sleeves, again very conservative and proper. We got along well and had a pleasant dinner.

I drove her back to her place after dinner. She invited me up for a drink. That's positive, I thought and I was curious to see her place.

"Can I offer you a drink?" Christa asked as we walked into her lounge.

"Oh, I've got to drive so I'll have a tea, no milk please." I said.

"How about a wine? I'm going to have one?

"No thanks, Christa. Tea is fine."

I sat on her large couch and she brought in a tray and sat down right next to me. I smelled her perfume for the first time -- a very subtle gardenia like scent.

Christa placed her face close to mine and I kissed her and could feel her excitement building.

"You are a very romantic lady - "

I couldn't finish my sentence as she pushed me down on the couch then jumped on top and straddled me. This prim, proper, take her home to meet your parents lady, was now wild eyed, laughing and aggressively unbuttoning my shirt.

We made love. Afterwards, I told her how amazing I thought she was.

"I enjoy making love. But we haven't had any real love making yet. Have you ever sensually made love so strong you lose track of space and time?"

"Yes...of course." (I stopped myself from saying, "Oh, yeah, I make love like that every morning and every night. Yep... sure do. All the time...).

Christa went wide eyed at my nonchalance response.

"My ex-boyfriend and I would have groped each other in the restaurant. Have you ever flashed to your partner in public?"

I laughed. This was getting interesting.

"Tell me more, Christa."

"When we were in the restaurant, I was looking for a dark corner where we might make love. Have you ever had made love in public, or in a retail dressing room (she named a well-known retail department store), or made love in a hotel with all the curtains and blinds wide open, or on the balcony?"

"Ahh...no." I said.

"Oh come on.... Have you made love on the beach?"

"You mean on the beach at night?"

"Anytime?"

"Oh, well let me think. Does making love in a public swimming pool count?" I asked.

"Only if other people are in the pool."

"Haha!" I was laughing out of control. "You are very cool, Christa. My life is dull. Did you wear out your last boyfriend?"

"Silly boy. I'll educate you."

We continued to make love that night.

The next morning, my body was aching from straining muscles I didn't know I had. I left moving very slowly.

Christa would make a great partner for an adventurous guy; and I want to read her book if she writes one.

Dee's comments on Christa:

Women complain you can never please men, and now I can see why. I'm sure you said on your profile you wanted a woman with a sense of adventure. It's not Christa's fault you were thinking travel, sailing, scuba diving etc.

Wholesome, conservative Christa sounds like the dream woman, the girl next door type. The minor detail that she'd insist you made love at midday against the front yard fence, astride the letter-box, beside the BBQ the neighbors are trying to cook on....

You really should think positive!

-Dee

"As a rough rule of thumb, I would say the smaller the pond the more belligerent the fish.
-Craig Brown

Chapter 14. PETER

At first sight, I was most impressed with Peter. He was tall, sophisticated and very elegantly dressed. He bought me a coffee and we began to chat. He was apparently still getting over his marriage break-up, as this was the first topic he brought up. I was a little disconcerted by this, and felt it wasn't a good sign.

He mentioned they had another home in Tuscany, and various other properties around the world but these had been split between them as a result of the marriage settlement, and he seemed rather bitter about it.

I changed the topic of conversation to some of the things he'd mentioned on his profile, such as art, and he picked up on this and asked about my love of cooking, which I'd mentioned on mine. He told me he loved food, but his wife had done all the cooking during their marriage.

He seemed keen to meet again, so I gave him my phone number and later received a text to say he'd be in touch the following week.

We did meet up again and went to the movies and then on to dinner. I offered to pay half, and he was quick to accept this. Our conversation flowed easily and we seemed to have many common interests, so I enjoyed the evening. Peter suggested we meet again the following weekend. He had mentioned his love of art, and invited me to meet him at his apartment in the centre of the city so I could see his paintings.

His home was beautiful, with wonderful furnishings, antiques and soft Turkish rugs, and fine paintings covered the walls.

We spent the day visiting art galleries, where he was greeted by name on almost every occasion. He was obviously well known to the gallery dealers.

A jarring note during the course of our dates was his frequent, negative comments about Asians, as there are a number of them living in our city. It was apparent he was quite racist, a quality that doesn't impress me.

We met again the following weekend, as he'd suggested another movie and then dinner at his place. It was rather amusing, as he'd told me at our first meeting that he didn't know how to cook, yet when dinnertime came, he pulled a partly consumed fish pie from the refrigerator. He said 'a friend' had given it to him. It was obviously leftovers from the previous night, and I guessed an earlier date had hoped to impress him with her cooking.

This didn't worry me too much, but I was less than impressed when he served up the meal, as he'd filled my plate almost solely with mashed potatoes from the top of the pie, whilst his contained all the fish!

Peter then turned his back to fill our wine glasses, but I could see he poured my wine from one bottle, his from another. It appeared the more expensive wine was not to be wasted on me...

By the end of the evening, any interest I had had in Peter was fast waning. As he walked me to my car, we had to make our way through a large crowd, and as we did so a young Chinese guy, chatting over his shoulder to his friends, cut in front of Peter. To my horror, Peter deliberately shoulder charged him, whilst muttering something derogatory about Asians. The poor young man apologized, whilst his friends and I stood open mouthed at Peter's rudeness.

I didn't see Peter again, as by this time I'd decided the 'fish pie' lady was more than welcome to him!

Bruce's comments on Peter:

Dee, in my view, Peter is not a bad guy. You must consider that fact that Pete just went through a divorce and now longer owns properties he worked very, very hard for?

His ex-wife may have run away with an Asian man and Peter might be pigeon-holing millions of Asian men as wife stealers?

Pete's wife may have done all the cooking. He may not have been used to being in the kitchen and probably thought it was polite to serve the top of the pie first?

Somebody must have a long talk with Peter to get to the bottom of it all and that could - still be you? My advice is to invite him to dinner at your home and you do the cooking. Why not cook a fish pie for him and show him how to serve it?

If he still grabs all the good parts for himself, put a strong laxative in his dessert and serve it to him saying, "I hope everything comes out all right in the end with you and the nice lady who made the fish pie for you before."

Best to you Dee.

-Bruce

"People tend to put entertainers on pedestals. We're human beings, just like you. You may see us smiling, and whether we have money or not, we still have bills to pay, we still have our stresses. I think a lot of people want to focus on others' shortcomings to make themselves feel better. And it's a very sad thing."
- Janet Jackson

Chapter 15. CHRISTINE

Christine worked as a dancer/entertainer in a gentlemen's club in Orlando, Florida. I didn't meet her online. My brother and I and some friends went on a golfing holiday trip to Orlando, Florida. We played golf during the day and hit the nightclubs at night.

At the Gentlemen's Club, known as "Goddesses on Parade," we found seats and a small table right below the elevated runway. I was sitting up against the runway, just next to the curtain where dancers come out to begin their routine. We were laughing, having drinks and talking with amazement about the gorgeous dancers entertaining us.

Marvin Gaye's "Sexual Healing" began to play, then gradually grew louder, and louder and when it was booming out, I glanced up at the runway and the curtains opened. My eyes widened at the sight of a large-breasted, blue eyed blonde wearing a nurse's cap. Strutting out with her uniform half open and a stethoscope hanging down from her neck, and wearing no pants except for a tiny G string, Christine began her routine.

Awestruck and straining to see every move she made, I clumsily fell out of my chair in front of this gorgeous woman. The rest of our group were laughing out of control.

Totally embarrassed, I scrambled back to my seat. Christine saw me tumble out of my chair and decided to have some fun with me.

She stopped dancing and bent towards me, then motioned me to stand up. Obediently, I stood up, eye level with two beautiful large breasts bouncing away (saying hello to me) about six inches from my embarrassed red face.

A huge smile formed on my red face. I stuck my chest out as far as I could. Then Christine slowly began to unbutton my shirt -- all the way down. Pressing the stethoscope to my chest, she began fanning her face indicating to the crowd my heart was racing out of control. The crowd was now cheering me on!

Christine didn't stop there. With her navel a little bit below my face, she grabbed me by the ears with both of her hands and slowly rubbed my face over her heavily perfumed G String! The crowd continued to cheer! My brother and friends couldn't breathe they were laughing so hard! When she was through with me, she went through finished her dance routine blowing a kiss to me as she left the stage.

The next dancer came on stage and began her act. Christine came out the side door with a small cape on and sat down next to us. My brother bought her an overpriced ginger ale. We talked to Christine and she told us she'd been doing the nurse routine for a year and was looking for other work, being tired of the nightlife. We continued talking for 20 minutes. She finished her drink, and as she was leaving us to visit with other patrons, I asked her to have dinner with me.

Surprisingly, Christine turned and agreed and gave me her card and told me she was free tomorrow evening.

I picked her up at her apartment. She came out her front door, transformed into an everyday office girl you wouldn't even notice on the street. She hid her amazing figure behind a conservative dark blue dress and a light evening jacket. We went to a Japanese Restaurant on International Drive.

"I don't get asked out much." She said.

"Yeah, I gathered most of the girls work late."

"Dancing is totally time-consuming and there's no social life."

"Christine, I'm not sure I know how to phrase this question, and please don't take any offense, but you are totally gorgeous on stage, yet...now you look like a Pollyanna Office Girl – so to speak – "

"I like to blend in." She interrupted.

I felt totally stupid. Of course, she wants to blend in. She was used to men going crazy over her almost every night. I shook my head and said, "Yeah, I understand."

We talked about her life goals. She wanted to settle down with the right man in the Orlando area. Since I was from out of town I didn't see much future with her. I assumed Christine went out with me for a change of pace as even a glamorous life dancing to a raving crowd gets boring as anything does.

Her father was an engineer and she had a normal upbringing. As we continued to give each other our histories, there was a pause in the conversation. I was silently trying to figure out how I could manage the large distance between us to date her further.

Christine broke the silence with, "Why did you ask me to dinner?"

"I just thought you were totally cool and a great person to get to know." I said.

"I am. I've met a lot of people, mostly from Orlando. Guys ask me out all the time but I shy away."

"So why did you agree to go out with me? Hey, I'm not putting myself down but I'm a bit older than you and there were plenty of great looking younger guys wanting to take you out."

"You just seemed nice. I got a nice feeling from your smile. I liked your friends too."

Yeah, girls seem to trust older men at times. I wasn't sure why. Perhaps they just like to be treated well? I didn't know. I laughed at myself for taking her out to dinner since I wasn't sure what I was doing. So, I lightened it up.

"I don't think I'm going to hear the end of it with the nurse routine you did on me! They're still laughing. You were great and you brought the house down." I said.

"Yeah, I do that routine if the right guy is sitting where you were. It's all fun." She said.

"How can you tell if the 'right guy' is sitting in that seat?"

"I just get a feeling by looking at who's sitting there. But one night, I chose the wrong guy who started to come up on stage and the bouncers had to throw him out."

"Haha! I wish I would have seen that." Christine was beaming with pride at her entertaining abilities. I wanted to know more about her. I was curious.

"May I ask what you earn per week?" I asked.

"Oh, I make a good living if I don't spend it all."

"I understand what you mean – it's so easy to spend. So, tell me about your past relationships? I'm surprised you haven't got a tall dark and handsome guy escorting you around?"

"Oh, I lived with a guy for two years but the hours of my work made it difficult to have anything last.

He worked during the day and we only had an evening or two a week to share. He met somebody else and off he went."

She excused herself to the ladies' room. Time to reflect on this, I thought. I couldn't move to Orlando and give up friends and relatives. Christine didn't want to move anywhere. This was a dead end but an enjoyable evening.

I asked the waitress to take a few pictures of us. My friends wouldn't believe this was the same girl. I wished Christine well and we ended the evening. I took her home and we exchanged goodbyes. We didn't see each other again, but our one date was a lot of fun.

Dee's comments on Christine:

Christine sounds like a nice girl, and a lot of fun.

-Dee

"I'm probably one of the most dangerous men in the world if I want to be. But I never wanted to be anything but me."
- Charles Manson

Chapter 16. STEPHEN

Stephen seemed worth meeting when first I read his profile. He had spent 23 years living in Europe and Australia and returned home a few months previously. He was now living in the same city as me, just a couple of streets away. I thought how convenient this would be if we should get along and start dating.

We met for coffee and he immediately began to tell me about his marriages – three in total. This was a little surprising, but I settled in, prepared to listen to his story.

Stephen told me his first wife had ruined his reputation by telling people in the community he hit her, which he claimed was completely untrue.

"I worked hard all through the marriage," he said, "so my wife took off with someone who worked for me".

"That must have been devastating for you", I replied, trying to be sympathetic but already thinking it was possibly a very wise thing for the wife to do.

"Do you diet?" Stephen suddenly enquired.

"Um, no, actually" wondering if he meant I should.

"My wife was only 52kg. She was always dieting and going to the gym. I should have known she was looking for someone else. She ruined me in the community, you know, by telling everyone I beat her" he repeated. "She told them that as an excuse for having an affair."

I couldn't quite make out what dieting had to do with anything, but decided to let him continue. The second wife had apparently died, it wasn't clear why, and then Stephen moved on to the third wife's story.

"She was slightly nutty" Stephen affirmed. "She would get upset over the silliest things."

"Such as?"

"Well, we had an argument, and I told her my friend Pete asked me what I saw in her."

I could quite understand her being upset if he was silly enough to tell her something like that.

"And then what happened?"

"Well, she grasped my shoulders and shook me. I grabbed her wrists and thrust her away. She did it again, so I pushed her. She decided not to stop herself, and fell through the door. I had to call an ambulance as she'd cut her head, and smeared it all around to make it look worse. It was all her fault; she didn't put her foot back to stop herself."

I think my mouth was hitting my knees, I was so astounded anyone could be so obtuse and lacking in any sense of responsibility.

"Weren't you arrested?" I gasped.

"Nah" he replied. "I took off before they got there, and split the country. That's why I came home. Now I'm looking for someone nice to settle down with." He looked at me expectantly. "So what about you? Do you live near here?"

"Oh no, no!" I exclaimed. "I just shop here occasionally. Oh, goodness! Is that the time? It's been lovely meeting you, but I have to dash, I must pick up my granddaughter from school." I lied.

"You haven't told me anything about yourself. Would you like to meet again?" Stephen asked.

I pretended not to hear, and just gave a bright wave as I headed for the door. Fortunately, I haven't encountered Stephen again in my neighborhood, but I'm looking over my shoulder just in case.

Bruce's comments on Stephen:

Not cool to hurt a woman. Not ever cool to hurt a woman who weighs 52 kg. Better to hug her than push her away. Glad you got out of there.

-Bruce

"Holding on to anger is like drinking poison and expecting the other person to die."
- Buddha

Chapter 17. ROBERTA

I enjoyed reading Roberta's profile. Having average looks and a great taste in clothes, she worked as a court reporter pounding away on a steno machine every day. She'd been divorced and was looking to go through life with a partner, as I was.

Her downtown apartment was near the Courthouse and she asked me after our first 30 minute coffee meet-up to come over for dinner. I was surprised she invited me over to her apartment after one coffee. So, I asked her about it.

"Thank you very much for the invitation and I would love to come over for dinner. But, don't you think you should be careful who you meet online? Hey, you hardly know me and it's good to be cautious?"

She didn't respond right away and sat back in her chair with a puzzled look on her face. Then smiled and said, "I think I'm a good judge of character."

"Well, yes I'd love to see your apartment and get to know you."

A few nights later, I went over to her apartment, and as I got off the elevator to her floor, I found her apartment door and knocked. She opened the door wearing a comfortable low white neck V-line top and a royal blue skirt which came down to an inch above her knees. A very attractive and sexy outfit, I thought.

The dinner she was cooking smelled great. She offered me a drink and we talked more about each other and she told me about her job and how court reporting can be boring and mundane.

"Don't you find criminal cases interesting?" I asked.

"I mainly do personal injury, car accidents and sometimes a divorce. Most of the time I'm transcribing how accidents happen, medical care, future medical care, lots of stuff about injuries."

We talked on and then had a nice dinner getting to know each other more. I was still wondering why she invited me over to her apartment without knowing me very well. After dinner, we settled back on a living room couch.

"Oh, excuse me, I haven't given you a tour of my place."

She got up and held out her hand and showed me around her apartment. The floor to ceiling windows dramatically showcased the downtown skyline. As we walked through, she'd point out various buildings.

We sat back on the couch and started to kiss and the kissing continued until she took me by the hand into her bedroom. She closed all the drapes and closed the door. The room went completely black.

I went with it and made love to her. I sensed it had been a while since she felt a human touch and affection and guessed I was the lucky guy in the right place at the right time.

After making love, I still couldn't see her - or my own hand in front of my face - and like most men, I enjoy visual stimulation. I asked her if we could turn on the light. She flicked a dim lamp on her nightstand.

"Will you stay the night with me?" She asked.

"Of course."

I went to the bathroom and she told me where to look in the bathroom vanity for toiletries I could use for the night and morning. When I came back to bed, our love making continued until we both were almost asleep. The total darkness bothered me.

"Why do you keep your bedroom completely dark?"

"I can't sleep if there's any light." She had to work the next morning and I respected that, so we talked briefly before going to sleep. Both of us were happy and relaxed, and we dozed off.

A few hours later, I woke up having to visit the bathroom. Roberta was sound asleep. I couldn't see the bathroom door. I slowly got up extending my arms out in front of me feeling for the end of the bed and crunched my right toe on the bed leg. I strained to muffle my cries of the exploding pain. Gritting my teeth, I slowly hobbled along, then stubbed the same toe on a dresser table leg. Excruciating pain, I muffled my agony, but I didn't let out a sound.

I could hear Roberta slowly breathing in her sleep. I continued hobbling and found the bathroom and quietly closed the door and searched for the light switch. As I was searching for the light switch, I bashed my toes on the bathtub. With my eyes watering from the pain, I found the light and sat on the toilet, totally amazed Roberta was still sleeping. With two toes bleeding, I cleaned my blood off the bathroom floor, then looked through her medicine cabinet for Band-Aids and couldn't help but notice she had a prescription for Zoloft.

I couldn't find Band-Aids, so I carefully wrapped my slightly bleeding toes in tissue and slowly hobbled back to bed.

We continued to date. We planned a movie together after she finished work on a Friday. I waited for her in her waiting room reading a magazine when I heard her burst out yelling at one of her co-workers like a banshee from hell. The yelling continued for five minutes. It sounded complicated, over a man they both knew. The inflections in Roberta's voice made it difficult to overhear what was being said. The co-worker wasn't saying much. Roberta was the one screeching and I realized I might be dating a "Dr. Jekyll and Ms. Hyde."

The yelling stopped all at once. Then a silence followed as I watched the door open. A woman walked out in tears.

Roberta followed a short time later and saw me sitting there.

"I've got a stop to make before the movie. Let's go."

I didn't say anything. It wasn't a normal angry mood she was going through.

She was another person - shrew like. Talking in short sentences, her face was contorted and she couldn't seem to snap out of it.

"Take a deep breath." I softly suggested. She didn't respond.

We stopped at a law office on the way to the movie and after Roberta nodded to the receptionist, she walked through the inner door like she owned the place. I could hear an angry discussion begin - but lower in volume. Then silence. She came out the door grim faced and off we went to the movie. I didn't say anything, but waited for her to say something. She was mainly silent shaking her head negatively when I asked her if she wanted any concessions for the movie.

She calmed down after the movie, but it was clear to me she had a temper.

"What was it with you and the young lady you were mad at?"

"Don't want to talk about it." She said.

"Okay, but what about the second stop. Who was that lawyer?" I asked.

"Don't want to talk about it."

If she didn't want to tell me, that's fine. Although I'm just guessing, it seemed the co-worker and the lawyer were in a relationship and perhaps Roberta was in a prior relationship with the lawyer, or a spin-off of that?

I didn't date her further but hope she's doing better.

Dee's comments on Roberta:

Yes, we've all met Roberta, the one who is charm personified to anyone they want to impress, and hell on wheels to anyone who crosses them.

The reason she keeps the bedroom so dark, Bruce, is to hide those vampire teeth that come out at night......

- Dee

"Once you start lying, you get kind of comfortable. You start believing it. Especially if you truly believe you didn't really cheat because you were doing what everybody else was doing."
— Tyler Hamilton

Chapter 18. DAVID

You know how sometimes you fall fast and hard for someone, then looking back, wonder what on earth you were thinking? That's how it was with David. I guess I tend to take people at their own evaluation, and David's opinion of himself was extremely high. He did have some justification, of course. He was very charismatic and charming, owned several extremely profitable businesses, moved in the best circles, was on first-name terms with various celebrities, and owned all the boys' toys you could imagine.

I loved it, of course, when David would drive up in his beautiful Bentley car, and take me to dinner at the finest restaurants in town. It was wonderful, too, to go out on the harbor in his gorgeous boat, and to be taken on holiday to luxurious resorts. Okay, I admit it, my head was turned, but oh! How I loved the lifestyle!

There were just a couple of little flies in the ointment that disturbed me, and one was how much David drank. I'm not keen on heavy drinkers, it always becomes a problem sooner or later, but I guess at the time I was looking through rose-colored glasses, and only seeing what I wanted to see. I ignored, or made excuses for David when he started to raise his voice at me, or became obnoxious to the staff he dealt with.

The other aspect I was becoming uncomfortable with was all the little white lies.

"No, no, I don't smoke, I hate that nasty habit." Yet he would come back after taking a phone call outside, with nicotine reeking on his clothes.

Or, "I haven't heard from the ex-wife in years, can't deal with the woman," but I'd seen photos of them both in various newspaper clippings on the Internet, and since recognized her leaving his office building as I was going in.

I unconsciously ignored these red flags, but the drinking became a real problem on my birthday. I became very nervous about David driving us after he'd demolished two bottles of red wine on his own, plus a couple of cocktails. To make it worse, David was becoming very obnoxious, and he started to abuse me for my supposed ingratitude.

"I try to give you a lovely evening, and all you can do is complain about my drinking!" David roared as the bellboy brought our car to the door.

"If you're going to carry on about it," he trumpeted, "then you can damn well drive." David sat himself in the passenger seat and promptly passed out.

I had no idea how to drive a Bentley, but the attendant had left the motor running and the lights were on, so I pulled gingerly out into the traffic. Though I was terrified of driving this expensive machine, I managed to safely make the drive back to David's home, and pulled into the garage.

The Bentley was keyless, and I had no idea how to turn it off. I sat with my foot on the brake, trying to figure it out, when David suddenly awoke and roared in my ear "Hit the brake! Hit the brake!"

I nearly leapt out of my skin, and without thinking, hit the accelerator!

If you're a car lover, then read no further......

The beautiful Bentley leapt forward, and demolished the wall in front. Even worse, the car ploughed straight through into the bathroom of a guest bedroom! Water from a demolished toilet fountained into the air, and cascaded over the car, while a bathtub slowly toppled against David's door.

My jaw dropped, I was frozen in horror, it was a situation completely outside my ability to cope. I opened the car door, turned to David, said "'Bye," then walked rapidly to my own car and drove away!

Amazingly, when David rang me a few days later, he simply asked why I had left, and never referred to the Bentley, or the demolished bathroom again. I certainly wasn't going to raise the subject!

Our relationship faded a short time later, however, when David invited me on a short trip overseas with another couple. His home was closer to the airport than mine, so we'd arranged to meet there. It was quite early in the morning, before the housekeeper arrived, and I was rather surprised, just before we left David's house, to notice wineglasses on either side of his bed.

The mystery was solved however, when leaving the resort to return home, I overheard David telling his friend a hilarious (in his view) story about how he'd been entertaining his ex-wife in bed, when his ex-mistress arrived and banged on the door.

Apparently the two women had a major screaming argument, while David enjoyed the show.

I decided this was a situation I, for one, was happy to bow out of, but I'm sure David is still charming his way through life.

Bruce's comments on David:

I like David. Drinking, smoking, being obnoxious…a lot of men like to do these activities because they are fun and help ease daily pressures although they tend to make your health go into the toilet like the Bentley. Roberta would straighten him out.

Very fortunate too neither of James' exes was sitting on the pot in the guest bathroom when you said hello with his Bentley.

-Bruce

"True love comes quietly, without banners or flashing lights."
- Erich Segal

Chapter 19. JANET

As, I've said before in my previous book, "I Came, I Saw, I Coffeed," I was getting tired of dating and wondered what was wrong with me to date so much and meet so many women. I found the "It's just a game of numbers" theory turned out to be a "game of confusion" with so many wonderful women out there.

My grandmother was right when she told me there will be women you will like who won't like you, and the women who like you, you won't like.

My grandmother passed away. At her funeral reception, I took a break and went to the coffee area where Janet, a friend of my cousin's, was standing talking with my cousin. I could tell when Janet glanced at me I made a nice impression on her. I started talking with her and learned she was a young widow and after talking with her for ten minutes, I asked her out and I wasn't sure why. Janet just seemed normal and pleasant and I was curious to learn more about her. Her husband had passed away two years earlier.

On our first date, there weren't fireworks going off in my head and no strong chemistry either. There wasn't anything special about her. She dressed normally, nothing flashy, had average looks and I didn't know how things would develop.

We went to dinner and she asked me about myself and I gave her my full history in detail – something I hadn't ever done before. I was a workaholic and didn't pay much attention to my wife and came home trying to just simply unwind. My ex-wife, on the other hand, had things she needed to discuss and she knew issues were the last thing I wanted to hear. This led to many arguments, of course.

My ex-wife decided without telling me she was going to divorce me and had it planned with lawyers and I fell into her web of escape which left me with a distrust of women.

I asked Janet to tell me her history. She didn't say anything exciting or unusual, just related her average good life to me which was abruptly broken up by the sudden death (heart attack) of her husband. Her friends helped her through it. She wasn't looking for a permanent partner but agreed to go out with me out of curiosity and something to do. She clearly understood what I and my ex-wife went through and told me she didn't want to get involved with me unless I could somehow forgive my wife for divorcing me.

That surprised me and I wasn't sure I could do that. I thought at first not to go further with her. We'd just met and she wanted to change my way of viewing my past and forgive someone who (in my view) caved in our world?

Deep down, I knew Janet was right.

Janet seemed to understand my past very well. Other women I had met didn't want to know deep personal things. Yet, I somehow, for some unknown reason, felt comfortable in confiding in her on our first dinner date. Perhaps, my subconscious was telling me to trust this woman. There was something about her that made me open up. Most other women were more concerned about their own lives, or just wanted to know where they would be nesting and what to expect. Janet was the only one who somehow got me to spill my guts.

Dinner became secondary as we talked on and on and without realizing it, several hours had passed. I knew she was right in her view and highly respected her for not wanting to go further with me having this issue.   I think most other guys would just simply forget about Janet then and there. I told her I would think about it and we continued to date.

I didn't think I would fall in love with her but I did. She understood my nature and vice versa. It was a naturally growing attraction. There wasn't anything special either of us did to enhance our relationship. When we talked, her replies and my replies fit almost like puzzle pieces - effortlessly fitting together. We began to live together. Living alone had been fine with me. I read that if a person is happy with themselves they are comfortable living alone. I am happy with myself but sincerely feel I am a better person living with someone to love. Solitude can lead to problems as a mind that isn't fed with interest in another person, begins to feed on itself. Life became better balanced with her.

I reflected on what people mean when they talk about "falling in love" when you least expect it. Janet's understanding, comfort and communication made her become a beautiful and irreplaceable person in my eyes, greater than any women I'd ever met.

As I've said before, to me, "Falling in love" means "falling" because you don't force yourself to fall, you just fall into it.

Dee's comments on Janet:

I suspect, Bruce, if you had met Janet when first you began to date, you would have dismissed her advice to forgive your wife as impossible. Janet is a very smart, strong woman. You were so lucky to meet each other when you'd arrived in a space where you could be receptive to her wisdom.

I wish you long life and happiness together.

- Dee

"I have always been delighted at the prospect of a new day, a fresh try, one more start, with perhaps a bit of magic waiting somewhere behind the morning."
- J. B. Priestley

Chapter 20. MICHAEL

It's easy to gently laugh at the idiosyncrasies of the men I've dated, but I can't help but realize they didn't get the dating goddess they may have been expecting, either.

When I first started dating again in my fifties, I was looking forward to meeting one of those Mills and Boons romantic heroes I just knew were out there. I forgot for a while that people are simply human beings, with flaws and vulnerabilities, not perfect characters with spotlessly correct scripts, written on a blank page.

Instead, forgetting, (if ever I knew how) to be fun, frothy and flirtatious, when first meeting men, I suspect I grilled my poor suitors as though they were robbery suspects under a blinding spotlight. 'Name, rank, and serial number?' I would enquire, beady-eyed, primed for information on their past history, prospects and/or penury before they barely had time to raise a coffee to their lips. Frozen like rabbits in the headlights, they spluttered their best answers, fearing (or hoping like hell!) they'd fail the test, and praying for escape.

Being a slow learner, it took me a long while to realize why the men I liked and really enjoyed meeting were never to be heard from again. On the other hand, those I immediately dismissed as being of no interest whatsoever, phoned, texted or asked for another date within minutes of our first meeting.

Eventually the penny dropped. If I liked a man, I very much wanted to know more about them, whether we had any common interests and whether they felt any attraction to me. On the other hand, when someone wasn't a match, I relaxed and chatted to them quite casually, which immediately made them like me because they relaxed too. Oh, to go back and do it all again! Well, with the ones I liked, at least.

In spite of this, I did meet my Prince Charming in the end. Well, not quite in the end, because Michael was actually the very first man I dated from the Internet. He wasn't one of the high flyers I later met, but was a very tall ex policeman, now working as Head of Security for a major company. When we first met, he was very smartly dressed, and I loved his sexy English accent. He told interesting stories of his career, and was amusing, intelligent and a gentleman. I found he was kind and gentle, and I couldn't have hoped to meet a nicer man.

The only drawback was that Michael lived a two hour drive away, and over time this really caused him a problem. He refused to let me do the driving, and in spite of my protests, before our dates, preferred to drive home, an hour from his work, to shower and change, before heading into town to meet. It was difficult to do anything on the spur of the moment, because of the distance factor, and eventually, just before Christmas one year, Michael told me he was finding the distance factor too hard and that regretfully he wanted to end our romance.

I was devastated, but was unable to change his mind. We did, however, continue to meet for a catch up now and again, so our friendship continued.

A few years later, Michael contacted me again. He offered to take me to dinner, and said he had something to ask me. He didn't raise the subject over dinner, and I wondered what on earth it could be.

Michael drove me home and of course I invited him in, but he stopped me as I opened the car door, and asked me to close it, as he wanted to ask his question in the darkness. Michael told me then that he had been a fool, and made the biggest mistake of his life when he ended our relationship, and asked if I'd consider seeing him again.

Would I? Well, what do you think? It had taken my lovely man so long to realize what we had was special, but now, finally, he'd come to his senses. We eventually worked it out and after buying a home mid-way between our jobs, moved in together, and have been very content.

And so, dear readers, I did get my happy ending after all – after many, many coffee dates.

Bruce's comments on Michael:

Bravo! Best of love, luck and happiness to you Dee!

-Bruce

Mothers are the necessity of invention.
- Bill Watterson

Chapter 21. THINGS YOUR MOTHER NEVER TOLD YOU *(Internet Dating For the Unsuspecting)*

Internet dating can be very exciting but it can also be intimidating. Many over 50 are reluctant to try, so we thought some suggestions might be of help.

FIND A DATING SITE

Firstly, why not follow the Nike slogan, "Just Do It." Don't think about it too much, just find a dating site for mature men and women in your area and register. It may be best for you to research reviews of the dating site on Google or watch informational You Tubes about the site. If you have friends on dating sites, ask them about the dating sites they chose. Make sure it's a reputable site, of course, and be careful with your personal information. Most sites offer a free service so you can ease into it and begin by reading the profiles of others.

When you do a search for potential dates, search in your own area but broaden your age range. If you are say 50 years old, search for a partner from 45 to 50. On your second search, search in an age range of 50 to 55. On your third search, search in a range of 55 to 60. If you see someone who interests you during your searching, send them a smile or a message that you are interested in them such as simply, "I read your profile and you interest me. Please tell me more about yourself and let me know if my profile interests you." Or, message him or her, and simply ask if they are interested in meeting you for a coffee at a convenient time and place. ☐

Tell yourself you must act to meet someone. It's not going to happen unless you do something about it. ☐

SETTING UP A PROFILE

Once you've decided to join a dating site, the next step is to write your profile, and put up some good photos of yourself. This can be a bit difficult at first, as most of us aren't accustomed to writing anything about ourselves.

From the male point of view, Bruce believes women should not be overly concerned with their personal appearance. Although most men want to see a picture of an attractive person, it's good not to overdo it by posting a younger looking picture of yourself. Men have a saying about online dating, "If you don't look anything like your picture, you're buying me drinks until you do."

Just try to post the best possible picture(s) of yourself. Maybe have a friend help you chose the pictures. Remember, people can often look different when you meet them in person and most people aren't overly concerned about what a woman or a man looks like, as generally mature people want someone they can sincerely trust and enjoy talking to or just someone they simply get along with. □

Choose your best shots, but we would suggest you don't use professional photos, with full makeup and immaculate hair, if that's not how you're going to look when first you meet. If possible, it's good to have a second full-length photo.

Men, on the other hand, need to think twice about photos of themselves holding fish, guns, or assorted dead animals. You might think this makes you look like a good provider, or a fishing/hunting guide, but animal-loving women sometimes just think 'blerch' and move on to a more sensitive guy.

Your profile should reflect you, your interests and what you're looking for. Bear in mind though there are not too many men interested in macramé, or painting dolls' faces etc, so try to identify something that might lead them to say 'I'd like to talk to her about that'..... And men, your undying interest in your stamp/gun collection isn't really going to cut it. Some things are best glossed over or discussed later.

Don't lie about your age, even if you think you look younger. It's best not to say 'My friends tell me I look younger." Your friends are lying. What else do you expect them to say – "Sorry Pete/Margo, I think you look 100"?

There was a time when people felt the internet was another world, but now people realize it's a tool that we use in this world.
- Tim Berners-Lee

Chapter 22. YOU HAVE AN INTERNET PROFILE, NOW WHAT?

In the early days of Internet dating, people would message back and forth for months, getting to know each other. And how misleading this was! The persona that comes across in writing may be totally different from how we are face to face.

One man explained it by saying "Some people are very witty, with very clever ripostes, but when you meet them face to face, you find it takes them hours to come up with these responses". Ahem. (Looks away, whistling).

People now seem to meet after only a short exchange of messages, to establish much earlier whether there is any attraction and the all-important chemistry.

You may find you get messages or smiles etc from people who don't interest you. Some inoffensive and polite responses are:

"Thanks for saying hello, but I don't want to take things further right now. All the best with your search."

"Thank you. All the best with your search."

"Thank you, but I'm only looking for someone local."

"Thanks. I don't want to take things further right now as I'm a bit overwhelmed with contacts."

If they persist after your response, you are under no obligation to reply again. Either ignore their messages or block them.

A bachelor's life is no life for a single man.
- Samuel Goldwyn

Chapter 23. OH, WE ACTUALLY HAVE TO MEET?

So, assuming you've been corresponding with someone and are looking forward to meeting, what now?

Some people like to talk first on the phone, others are uncomfortable with this. If you agree to do so, it's best to only give out a cell-phone number, rather than your landline number. Avoid giving out more information than you are comfortable with.

For women, a priority to remember when meeting, is keep safe. We generally found it best to arrange a coffee meeting, or a drink at a bar, just somewhere very public. Never agree to meet at your home, or to get in a car with a stranger.

It's not too hard to chat for half an hour to someone new, and that's usually plenty of time for you to establish whether there's a connection. Committing to a dinner date for a first meeting can be too overwhelming, you may find yourself longing to leave before the first course has even arrived.

Don't make a quick judgment about the other person. Let the meeting progress and try to relax as best you can. You've got nothing to lose by forcing yourself to spend a little bit more time. You might find something interesting or learn of a mutual friend. ☐

The usual advice, when you meet someone new, is just be yourself, but bear in mind the very good counsel we so much wish we'd heard before beginning to date: If you were selling a house, would you point out all the faults to the prospective buyers? This is not the time to trot out "Apparently, I snore really badly" or "I don't get on with the people I work with" or "My kids are really such a problem!" or "The area I live in is so rough".

Don't talk negatively about yourself or others. There are enough bad things in the world that can happen to you and you don't need to remind anyone. It's best not to talk about your ex. It's fine to admit to having one, but leave it there, this is not the time to rant about him/her the way you might do to your friends (who are undoubtedly thoroughly sick of hearing about it, by the way).

Men, in particular, often don't have the opportunity to unload to friends, the way women do, but remember the man/woman you are meeting is hopefully your new lifetime partner, not your counselor.

Look for things you like, rather than being critical, keep your thoughts positive until you're really sure they're not the one you're looking for. It's an opportunity to meet new, exciting people and learn good things about them and their world. Keep the conversation light and fun, flirt a little. You may have forgotten how, but now is your opportunity to practice. Keep smiling and enjoy yourself!

It's very important for a man to listen to a woman. It's a tough world out there and men usually have logical responses popping up in the brain to solve an issue you might have. Bruce said it took him a while to understand this, but he realizes now it's important to listen to understand a woman's feelings and show sympathy and that you care about her feelings. Understanding her emotions is better than suggesting a solution to correct an issue and feelings seem to be much more important to a woman than solving the issue.

Try to keep the first conversation balanced. Remember that you're both probably a bit nervous and people aren't themselves and sometimes over-talk. Try not to dominate the conversation and if the new person you're meeting is talking too much, make sure you first listen and understand what they are trying to say, and then say, "Would you mind if I interrupted you?"

You will usually get the response, "No, go ahead, I'm talking too much anyway." Then begin by talking about something they are talking about. Or ask a question to have him or her explain a point in what they are talking about. Or, interrupt with a story about yourself on the same subject.

If all else fails and you can't stop the other person talking, just say, "I'm sorry, I've got to go and we'll continue this conversation later sometime." See what kind of response you get and see if the other person realizes they are talking too much and how considerate their response is to you. □

*Body language is a very powerful tool.
We had body language before we had
speech, and apparently, 80% of what
you understand in a conversation is
read through the body, not the words.
- Deborah Bull*

Chapter 24. YOU EXPECT CONVERSATION TOO?

If you're male, and find you're
experiencing difficulty in having a
conversation with a woman, it's probably
because you haven't dated for a while. Did

you see the hit comedy film, "40-Year-Old Virgin," where Jay (Romany Malco) and David (Paul Rudd) tell Andy (Steve Carrell) how to talk to a woman?

Jay: "Now you need to learn how to talk with women. "Most men don't know how to talk to women.... Just ask questions. That's it."

Andy: "I get nervous and I lock up. I never know what to say."

Jay: "The key is you don't say anything. Make them talk."

Andy: "How do you do that?"

Jay: "Just ask them questions. Girls love talking. Let them."

Andy: "What if they ask me a question?"

Jay: "Then answer their question with a question."

David: "It makes you seem mysterious. You talk too much about yourself, it makes you look needy. Put them on the spot."

The three of them walk into a bookstore and see a pretty blonde working there putting books back on the shelf.

David shoves Andy toward her, "Now give it a try."

Andy walks timidly at first then raises his head and forces himself to walk confidently up to her.

Beth (the pretty blonde): "Can I help you?"

Andy: "I don't know. Can you?"

Beth pauses then smiles, "Are you looking for something?"

Andy: "Is there something I should be looking for?

Beth is afraid to tell him she doesn't know much about books and is put instantly on the spot. Andy, for the first time in his life, has the upper hand in the conversation with a woman.

Beth: "Ah, we got a lot of great new books in. It depends on what you like?"

Andy: "What do you like?"

Beth: "Me? I don't know."

Andy: "Do you know?"

Beth pauses, then smiles: "To tell you the truth, I don't read much. So, I can recommend a book. But I would be just…bullshitting."

Andy: "Thanks for not bullshitting me…?"

Beth: "And what's your name?"

Andy: "It's Andrew."

Beth: "Don't tell on me Andrew."

Andy: "I won't. Unless you want to be told on?"

Beth smiles admiring dorky Andrew very much. Andy turns and walks out confidently knowing he, for the first time in his life, finally made a great impression on a woman, a total stranger. Andy runs into Beth again later in the movie and goes home with her for a hilarious spa bath scene.

- from Judd Apatow's and Steve Carrell's, "40-Year-Old Virgin"

Guys, give this "Ask Questions" a try. Get a woman talking and you'll make a great impression.

This works both ways, so if women also give it a try, you'll undoubtedly find, if you haven't dated for a while, most men will open up when you show him respect and appreciation for what he has done in his life. So be interested and appreciate his accomplishments no matter what they may be. It will ease him into talking about other subjects and to pay more attention to you.

When you really don't like a guy, they're all over you, and as soon as you act like you like them, they're no longer interested.
- Beyonce Knowles

Chapter 25. I FEEL SO REJECTED *(Sob)*

So would you like to meet again? How to go about it? The usual method in our experience seems to be for the man to text, message or phone within a couple of hours of the coffee date to suggest meeting again.

However ladies, if you don't hear immediately from him, there's nothing wrong with texting or messaging to say you enjoyed the meeting and would enjoy doing it again, but leave it there if you don't hear back. He's not busy with work or family, he hasn't lost your number, he isn't under the impression you weren't interested in him. He just doesn't want to meet again. Accept it and move on.

You may meet someone you feel a wonderful connection with, only to never hear from them again. Rejection is very hard for anyone to deal with, if you feel a strong connection but the other person doesn't. You begin to wonder what you said/did wrong. Don't worry, it's most often them, not you!

There can be a multitude of reasons two people don't feel the same connection. He/she may have just met someone else they're excited about, they may not have got over a previous relationship, there could be something going on at work that needs focus or there is a family issue to be resolved, who knows what?

One beautiful, very young-looking friend of ours couldn't understand why she hadn't been asked for a second date by a guy she very much liked, only to receive a belated message from him. He said she resembled his daughters so much, he would feel uncomfortable dating her!

Someone once described rejection as being in the wrong windows of time – you're standing at one window; the other person isn't at the same window. No matter how strongly you feel, it's best to put your big girl pants on and again, move on.

On the other hand, what to say when he/she is very keen, and you are not? It's just as hard to be the one doing the rejecting, but we've found people can generally accept a 'no'. It's not hearing anything at all that upsets them. A simple, effective message is "It was really great to meet you, but I'm looking for that elusive chemistry. I won't take it any further but I really enjoyed meeting you."

We've found this works okay, and it's kinder not to leave someone hanging.

Chapter 26. IF YOU GO DOWN IN THE WOODS TODAY... *(Scammers)*

Both men and women need to be very aware of, and beware of, scammers. Loneliness can be a trap that is so easy to fall into. Women, in particular, can find it very hard to accept the risk of losing that wonderful comfort a stimulating, exciting and joyous romantic correspondence can bring. Why? Because the dream will be lost and they know they'll have to return to the pit of loneliness.

Keep in mind, however, that pit is a lot deeper when all your money has been given to a scammer, to help him/her get out of jail, save a child, escape from the foreign airport, whatever their excuse may be for taking your money.

Any decent man or woman who loves you will borrow from friends and family, long before they'll take the risk of losing your regard by asking you for money. If anyone asks you for money, no ifs or buts, they're scamming, and it's time for you to once again move on.

Love is like a virus. It can happen to anybody at any time.
- Maya Angelou

Chapter 27. WE HAVE LIFT-OFF! *(Ideas on Easy and Creative First Dates)*

You've met, you like each other, and now you're ready for the real deal. First dates are an opportunity for a man and a woman to establish, or not establish a bond and to get know each other. So, these are our ideas on easy first "test the waters" dates.

Since it's usually up to the guy to decide on where to go on the first date, the best way to impress a lady is to show her you are interested in her and you want to get to know more about her. It is, of course, fantastic if you can pick out something to do she's passionate about. But if you're not sure what she likes or doesn't like, here are some suggestions:

A dinner theater gives an easy distraction to your conversation, especially comedies.

Conversation is important on the first date and it's nice to have a pleasant distraction like an easy listening music show. Dueling Pianos can be a lot of laughs.

A murder/mystery dinner train. You can both try to solve the whodunit and it's a lot of fun.

Women love beach walks at sunset. Drive to a beach, and take two beach chairs and a bottle of her favorite wine and watch the sunset.

If there is a Carnival nearby, take her to a Carnival. Ride the Roller Coaster, Ferris wheel, win something for her, and watch her relax and have some fun.

Take her bowling, drink beer, eat pizza and give her a big handicap and see if she can beat you. You could wager a kiss on each game or whatever comes to mind. If you keep beating her, increase her handicap each game.

Take her horseback riding. Women often love horses and most stables offer trail rides for beginners. If she hasn't ridden, but is curious about it, she should love the new adventure.

If there are vineyards in your area, take her on a wine tasting tour. Fine wines will make her relax and the conversation will flow easier with a few wines.

If she tells you she's a good cook, suggest having dinner at your place and cook her favorite dish together. Or, if you have a favorite dish, suggest she come over to show you how to cook it. Since it's your first date and you don't want to appear to be too fast with her, you might suggest a barbeque on a Sunday afternoon and do a Beer Can Chicken together or your favorite barbeque dish. Have drinks while you barbeque, of course. She'll feel good to teach you something and be impressed with your interest in her. It also gives her a chance to show off her cooking skills. If she can't cook, arrange a date where you can show off your own cooking skills. If you can't cook, try Googling "Easy recipes for bachelors to cook to impress a woman."

Take her to a ball game, football, basketball, hockey, roller derby, or any exciting event. If she's not a sport's fan, ask her to help you buy something for your sister's or daughter's birthday. If she's going to help you shop, you'll learn how she feels about money and the styles she likes. Decide on the right gift over lunch at the shopping center.

A movie, followed by dinner. Seeing the movie will give you something to talk about, avoiding awkward silences. A romantic comedy, or a foreign film, can be good options.

Go on a ferry ride, to a local beach. Maybe buy fish and chips, or an ice cream.

Take her to a pool bar, and teach her to shoot pool. If she's already better than you, she can teach you! Finish up with pizza and beer/wine nearby.

When was the last time you went to the museum? Explore the galleries, then have dinner at a little local nearby.

Art galleries are great too. Take her to the current exhibition, then argue about .... I mean, discuss, modern art at a nearby coffee bar.

Sign up for a cooking lesson, one where you eat the results. These are really fun, even if your best efforts turn out a disaster.

A picnic in a park, especially if there's music in the vicinity, is hard to beat. Grab a few items from your local bakery and supermarket, take a blanket, and don't forget the bottle of wine.

Lastly, there are restaurants that offer dining in darkness. You are supposed to judge the food solely upon its taste and texture. Since this is your first date, you are there to learn about each other regardless of personal appearance.

The tone of your voices, the topics of conversation will indicate to both of you how well you can communicate with each other. The novelty and fun of it all will make the conversation go easier and a memorable first date.

Grownups, as a rule, should always be ready to pay for their own meals - or else ready to graciously accept their date's insistence on paying. The point is, one doesn't sit there batting one's eyelashes, fully expecting someone else to claim the bill.
- Lynn Coady

Chapter 28. MONEY MATTERS

Who pays on a date? People over fifty were brought up in an era where it was customary for the man to pay for the woman. The downside of this is some men then had an expectation the woman owed them something i.e. sex. For a coffee date, this isn't going to be an issue, but be aware, times have changed. Neither of you should make any assumptions.

If going out to dinner etc ladies, it's easy enough to say "Shall we split this?" when the bill arrives and then do so if he agrees. If he wants to pay, let him and don't forget to thank him. That's all you're required to do.

One extremely wealthy man told us although he and his partner had been together for many years, and dined out every week, she always offered to split the bill. He never accepted, but loved the fact she didn't take it for granted he would pay.

*Eloquent speech is not from lip to ear,
but rather from heart to heart.
- William Jennings Bryan*

Chapter 29.
ICEBREAKERS FOR STALLED CONVERSATIONS

On the first meet, sometimes conversations stall and an intriguing question or comment is helpful. Try these simple questions - they will get the other person talking:

What was the best job you ever had?

What was the worst job you ever had?

What would be your dream job or business?

What is one thing you like about yourself?

What is the most important goal in your life?

What was the most difficult thing you've ever done in your life?

Tell me about your children (or grandchildren).

If you had three wishes, what would you wish for?

If you could live anywhere in the world where would you live?

If you could vacation anywhere in the world, where would you go?

If you could go back in time, who would you like to spend a day with?

What's your favorite food?

What's your favorite thing to do?

If you could invite two famous people to dinner, who would you invite?

When you were a child, what did you want to be when you grew up?

What was the most hilarious date you ever had?

What was your most embarrassing moment?

What's the favorite thing you like to do when you're alone?

Tell me two things you excel at.

Tell me one thing you hate to do.

What is the best compliment you ever received?

What is the funniest practical joke you ever played on anyone?

What is the funniest practical joke ever played on you?

What was the happiest moment in your life?

What was the saddest moment in your life?

What was the best advice on marriage you ever got?

What was the worst advice on marriage you ever got?

What is the greatest quality you like in a man (or a woman)?

Of all the things you can do in your life, what are you most passionate about?

Name one thing that drives you absolutely crazy.

What is the first thing you notice about someone when you first meet?

What was the absolutely best thing you've ever done in your life?

Sex is emotion in motion.
- Mae West

Chapter 30. MOVING ON TO INTIMACY

Ah, the after-50 difficult questions. Do you or don't you? If you do, when do you? If you want to, can you? And who with?

Most women seem to ignore the messages from anyone 25 years or more younger. And yes men, believe it or not, women get dozens of these messages, and pictures with and without clothes from horny young men. We'd suggest meeting any of these men/children probably won't actually do much for a woman's self-confidence or ego, so would be best avoided. Your choice, though.

Assuming you've met someone you'd like to establish a relationship with, the time will come, maybe sooner, maybe later, when you're really getting down to the nitty-gritty. Figure out if you're there for a frolic, or is this a good man or woman you want to share your life with?

We're not going to start giving you advice about safe sex, you probably know as much or more than we do.

Women tend to be hung up on showing their bodies, with all the lumps, bumps, wrinkles, fat and/or scars life has brought them. They can be terrified of making love with the light on. Men worry about erections, getting and/or losing them. They too have their own worries about how their bodies now look, and the pot-belly they're hoping you'll overlook.

The sexiest woman is the confident one, lying back saying "Come here, you lovely man, and let's have fun!" What man isn't going to desire a woman who thinks he's irresistible?

Men, older woman are quite able to cope with a lost erection, it isn't a big deal. You have other ways of satisfying her, and believe me, the comfort of lying in your arms can be the main feature. And since Viagra was invented, you have the option of a fall back position.

So, go forth and multiply! Oh, alright, maybe not multiply, but go forth and have a great time dating, and we'd love to hear your stories.

"Sex is part of nature. I go along with Nature."

-Marilyn Monroe

Chapter 31. WHY MEN WANT SEX and DON'T FEEL BAD ABOUT MAKING LOVE SO SOON.

Psychologist, Russell D. Clark III, PhD and Elaine Hatfield, Ph.D performed their famous study at Florida State University years ago where they had ordinary women approach random men and ask them the following question:

""I've been noticing you around campus lately and find you very attractive. Would you like to go to bed with me tonight?"

Keep in mind these women were not drop dead gorgeous and all of them just had average looks. They were dressed casually, no three inch spiked heels, no leather, no beauty queens, no plunging necklines, all were wholesome average looking women, approaching ordinary males on campus.

Ladies, do you think the men answered, "No Way! You're too forward for me?" Or, perhaps "I prefer to get to know you better before we have sex?"

The study showed 75% of the men said "Yes" and some of those men suggested "Why wait until tonight?"

By the way, those same psychologists did a later study where average looking men asked women at Florida State University the same question and absolutely none of the women agreed to have sex.

So, it's been scientifically proven men simply want sex. In the previous chapters Bruce wrote about women he had met on line where they perhaps made love too soon.

Over all, very few of the women Bruce met made love right away. Christa and Bruce did become intimate right away, but both clearly understood there were no strings attached. He wasn't going to make a promise and she didn't expect him to make a promise and vice versa. They both knew there were no strings attached.

In meeting women online, Bruce felt it was important, of course, to treat all women with respect and not to make promises he couldn't keep. If a man presses you to make love, you should ask him what his intentions are for the future. If he says he doesn't know or makes it clear to you no strings are attached to it, then you know he is being honest with you, since most heterosexual men just simply want sex as proven by the famous Clark and Hatfield study.

It's important to understand if you do decide to make love right away, it's not a bad thing. So, don't get down on yourself if you feel you made love too soon.

Women sometimes think "If I don't make love with him, he'll go away (not good if you really like him) and find someone else." Well, he may find someone else, but the one he'll stay with will be the one that he enjoys the most to be with and vice versa. The point is, men, simply by nature, enjoy sex and it's not a big deal if it happens quickly, so don't feel guilty about it.

Go on from there and learn about each other. Talk to each other and learn about each other's nature and enjoy the experience.

A final message to you from Dee and Bruce:

Thank you for reading and best to you and above all have fun meeting new people!

Thank you for purchasing this book. We hope you found it useful and entertaining and that our views gave you some insight into the seemingly complex world of relationships.

If you enjoyed reading it, please consider leaving a review on Amazon so more readers can find this title.

We wish you all the best if you are seeking a partner. We love questions or comments so don't be shy. If you're interested in our advice, please don't hesitate to ask.

Thank you again.
Kind regards
Dee Cleary and Bruce Miller
contactdeeandbruce@gmail.com

CPSIA information can be obtained
at www.ICGtesting.com
Printed in the USA
LVHW080535231120
672457LV00041B/1182

9 781540 489913